ALEXANDER ARCHIPENKO

Organized by

THE UCLA ART GALLERIES

With the following participating museums

CINCINNATI ART MUSEUM

COLORADO SPRINGS FINE ARTS CENTER

DALLAS MUSEUM OF FINE ARTS

FINE ARTS GALLERY OF SAN DIEGO

MUNSON-WILLIAMS-PROCTOR INSTITUTE,
    UTICA, NEW YORK

NATIONAL COLLECTION OF FINE ARTS,
    SMITHSONIAN INSTITUTION,
    WASHINGTON, D.C.

PHOENIX ART MUSEUM

WALKER ART CENTER, MINNEAPOLIS

WASHINGTON UNIVERSITY, ST. LOUIS

THE MUSEUM OF CONTEMPORARY ART
    OF CHICAGO

ALEXANDER

ARCHIPENKO

THE WARD RITCHIE PRESS

THIS EXHIBITION *is drawn in its entirety from the collection of Mrs. Alexander Archipenko. The UCLA Art Galleries and the other participating institutions wish to thank her for making the collection available, along with the papers of her husband, and the photographs, and in particular for her help in the preparation of the catalogue, and the clarification of the record.*

Thanks are due to Mrs. Katharine Kuh for her foreword, and for her personal recollections of the sculpture; and to Donald H. Karshan for his essay on the prints and drawings, as well as for the use of the archive on Archipenko which he has assembled.

The UCLA Art Galleries thank the UCLA Art Council for the generous support it has provided on this occasion.

FREDERICK S. WIGHT, *Director*
UCLA Art Galleries

TABLE OF CONTENTS

ALEXANDER ARCHIPENKO, the first sculptor of our century to recognize form as an illusion, investigated this mystery throughout his entire life. Almost from the beginning he became involved with the void, with perforated and concave planes, with what today we call negative form. Now, well over a half-century since his earliest experiments were initiated, we accept the fact that less can make more, that space can miraculously turn into form. What we occasionally forget is how much Archipenko was responsible for these intangible discoveries.

Long applauded as a pioneer Cubist sculptor, he was far more than that. He never merely transferred Cubist theories from painting to sculpture; he virtually invented his own kind of three-dimensional Cubism. Relying on the human body, preferably the female nude, as his point of departure, Archipenko constructed his figures with architectural precision, yet rarely sacrificed the rhythms of nature. His idealized women have the elongated elegance we sometimes associate with undulating plants, sometimes with those Gothic saints which echo the soaring churches they decorate. Archipenko confessed, "From the Gothic I learned to see the transformation of proportions as an . . . expression of the spiritual."

Unlike medieval sculpture, his figures are seldom frontal. They turn, twist, bend; they are inverted, foreshortened, and tautly poised. They move, yet more important—light moves over them with rippling speed. As early as 1912 Archipenko combined wood, glass, mirror, metal, canvas, and wire in dynamic constructions (or

15. Head (1913) 14⅞″

should we say assemblages) where light was manipulated with meticulous control, and where reflections and transparencies were deliberately exploited. A year or two later, again predicting present-day trends, he was already considering environmental groups.

But his greatest contribution was metaphysical. He made what is, seem what it is not. It was the duality of vision that interested him, less the image itself than our reaction to the image. Turning total voids into solid form, he also discovered that surrounding space could become as potent as dense mass.

Though Archipenko was widely acclaimed in Europe, he was never fully appreciated in America where he lived for thirty-four years. Coming here at the age of thirty-six and at the height of his European fame, he remained something of a displaced loner, a man who always seemed to be looking in from the outside. Moving from place to place, he restlessly pursued his roots, but they were not to be found in America. And, of course, during the early twenties, this country was scarcely ready for his sophisticated metaphors. Later, his ebullient color, admittedly more decorative than structural, disturbed American eyes which at that time were happier with restrained Gallic taste.

For, from beginning to end, Archipenko remained a Ukrainian, a man who often seemed closer to the near East than the West. The golden ornament and linear eloquence of Byzantium are so manifest in his work as sometimes to obscure its vigor. But, make no mistake, Archipenko belongs securely to the history of modern art, less because he reflected its influence than because he himself helped create it.

KATHARINE KUH

THE MEMORIAL RETROSPECTIVE EXHIBITION which is the occasion of this publication is drawn from the estate collection of my late husband's sculptures, drawings, and graphics. Some of the more recent works as well as works produced as early as 1908, here illustrated, are shown for the first time. The terra cottas and other works were considered too fragile to travel and could not be included—denying the exhibition and this publication much of the color with which my husband experimented. Color slides were made of twenty of the terra cotta sculptures, however, and their projection during the exhibition well serves to familiarize the viewer with this frequently used medium. Whenever possible bronze casts related to the colored works are shown.

Some of the terra cottas were produced in California. It seemed appropriate that the memorial exhibition originate in that state, for the time my husband worked and taught in California was always recalled with nostalgia. It was in California that he was able to produce and fire a life-size terra cotta, his largest, entitled MA (meaning in Hungarian the creative and mystic power in woman; not the colloquial English meaning for mother) which has the following inscription:

> "MA is dedicated to every mother; to everyone who
> is in love and suffers from love; to everyone who
> creates in the arts and in science; to every hero;
> to everyone who is lost in problems; to everyone
> who knows and feels Eternity and Infinity."

*Alexander Archipenko with his second wife,
Frances, showing her the lithographic
technique at St. Gallen, Switzerland,
March, 1963*

In 1960, when my husband and I were visiting in Paris, quite by chance we were informed that old friends of his, Monsieur and Madame Jean Verdier, had recently returned to France after many years in South America and that they still had stored in Cannes the plasters which had been left with them for safe-keeping when my husband had left France to go to Germany about fifty years ago. Bronzes from these newly-discovered plasters are in this exhibition. They are ADAM AND EVE, CROSSED ARMS, WOMAN (HEAD ON KNEE), WOMAN WITH CAT, SMALL RECLINING FIGURE, BLUE DANCER, BOXERS,[1] WOMAN COMBING HER HAIR (SEATED), and EGYPTIAN MOTIF. The bronzes, SEATED FIGURE and REPOSE, were cast from the terra cottas which also had been stored in Cannes. This is probably the first time that SEATED FIGURE as well as ADAM AND EVE and SMALL RECLINING FIGURE have ever been shown publicly. Of the more recent works, it should be noted that KING SOLOMON and SEATED WOMAN were never exhibited in the United States. KING SOLOMON had been conceived as a model in 1963 (see last photograph of Archipenko) for a sculpture sixty feet high, a project which never was pursued, but it is my hope it will eventually materialize, perhaps in America. The small recent version of FAMILY LIFE is also having its first showing in this exhibition. The early larger version of it which measured approximately six feet high was exhibited in the Armory Show and destroyed during World War I.

The European reaction to recent retrospective showings in Rome, Milan and Munich encourages me to believe in the

Last photograph of Alexander Archipenko in his New York studio working on plaster model of King Solomon, 1963

importance of keeping the comprehensive collection, which the memorial exhibition represents, as a *permanently intact group* so that it can be made available in perpetuity for viewing and research by artists, scholars and art enthusiasts. The Archives of American Art has just completed the microfilming of my husband's very extensive personal archive, a collection that will undoubtedly be of assistance to art historians. Several personal photographs from this group, hitherto unpublished, are reproduced in this publication. Donald Karshan's assistance in organizing and preserving the entire estate collection of objects and papers, his collaboration with the Archives of American Art, and his advice and efforts in connection with the memorial exhibition, have been invaluable. He is presently collecting widespread data for a *catalogue raisonné* of my husband's sculpture.

The memorial exhibition of sixty-seven sculptures represents approximately one-sixth of the presently known Archipenko *oeuvre*. Many of the early pioneering, and fragile, polychrome sculptures and "sculpto-paintings" (an expression coined by my husband[2]) are in public and private collections here and abroad.

Bearsville, New York
December 11, 1966
                                         FRANCES ARCHIPENKO

[1]This plaster of BOXERS is identical with the one from the Magnelli collection, now at the Solomon R. Guggenheim Museum. Both plasters are from the same mold, done in 1913.

[2]"Even though his first sculptures were inspired by the revolutionary theories, he showed immediately his strong personality by introducing an entirely new conception of sculpture. He gave the name 'Sculpto-Peintures' to reliefs generally made of plaster, carved and painted." Marcel Duchamp, Collection of the Société Anonyme, Museum of Modern Art, 1920. Case, Lockwood and Brainard, 1950.

59. Eagle (1959) 10½″ x 15½″

42. Torso in Space (1935) 8½″ x 27½″

To COURSE THROUGH THE WORK of Archipenko now that his chronology is complete and all his various inventions take on more cohesion is to rediscover an extraordinary genius. One must strive to understand the totality of his contributions, for his early conceptions re-emerged decades later, and it was obvious that they inspired him all his life. But then, if there was this fugue aspect, there was also great ultimate change. It is difficult to see his last work implicit in his first, and we must keep in mind how strange and bold his first things seemed at the time: his early and late works have their newness in common.

There were difficult times for him when the spate of creation slackened, years without immediate reward. Was it coming to America too early when there was no such ambiance of talent as the thirties and forties provided? Or was it disappointment over lesser acknowledgment in his new homeland? His precocious achievements were well behind him, yet he continued to refine and re-define them, even as his future sculptural intuitions were lurking in working drawings. There was some relation between his difficulty in offering and his audience's difficulty in accepting. Archipenko had a way of forcing reluctances upon us, as if for the pleasure of beating them down. For he was free of that conventional taste that has clung to the most revolutionary figures in Western art until just now, so that he could seem either too tasteful, or tasteless, and apparently not care. Perhaps he was so far outside our pervasive materialist faith (in his Eastern way) that his subtleties and dedications embarrass us without our knowing why.

Alexander Archipenko, Moscow, circa 1907/8

In the midst of such thoughts, one has the strange sensation that one is also rediscovering the 20th century that we still call "modern," and that everything now falls into place more simply. Cubism becomes more understandable, and less narrowly Picasso-Braque, a phase through which artists mysteriously passed. It becomes construction, the desire to invent or build, which is still very much with us. The early examples take on the look of the earlier Archipenko. (Even the NUDE DESCENDING THE STAIRCASE looks like an Archipenko for all its debt to photography.) It is not only Archipenko's early work which completes art history like the last piece in a puzzle (and immediately Brancusi's contribution is no longer eccentric), it is Archipenko's late work, with its wide range of materials, that comments on where we are now. The late Archipenkos are fresh and wonderful and again elucidate the contemporary.

Perhaps this exhibition, being in bronze, makes Archipenko's virtues more obvious. If the color is lacking, the forms stand clear. The fragile terra cottas and some of the large "sculpto-paintings" cannot travel, and bronze variants take their place.

Archipenko was twenty-one when he arrived in Paris in 1908. He was enrolled at the Beaux Arts for a matter of weeks. Actually, he went to school to the Louvre where he could plunge into the conglomerate past. "In my work from 1900 to 1910," he was to write in a truculent letter of a later date, "any intelligent connoisseur should find inspiration from such styles as Assyrian, Egyptian, Hindu, early Byzantine, Gothic, and Archaic Greek.

Alexander Archipenko and his first wife, Angelica, aboard the S.S. Mongolia in October, 1923, en route to their new life in the United States

From those are derived my thirty-year old style, not from the Negro or Picasso period." And, if so, then how Cubist is Archipenko? "I cooperated in creating it (Cubism) together with a small group of artists of whom I was the youngest. When I arrived in Paris this group was not organized as a unit. Only in 1910 was formed the Section d'Or." And Archipenko proceeds to list twenty-two members. Section d'Or was a confraternity.

It is true that many more things were happening than the Cubism that we think of now. Archipenko constructed; he worked with cylinders and elongated sections of cone, because metal bent that way, and with sheets of glass and with wood. In so doing, he followed more literally than others Cezanne's over-quoted statement that the sphere, cylinder and cone are the basic forms, that shibboleth of the Cubist.

To go back to a glimpse of Archipenko before he put on the armor of his style, he was born in Kiev in the Ukraine, the son of an engineer and inventor who taught at the university. He studied painting and sculpture in an art school in Kiev, went to Moscow and from there to Paris. His earliest work in Paris is instinctively mannerist and fluent—it is not surprising that Modigliani and Gaudier-Brzeska were attracted to his studio. His WOMAN WITH CROSSED ARMS (1908) is modeled with the facility of a Clodion, and he has been compared to Gian Bologna. As a young artist, he stated that Rodin's figures looked to him like those clinker-bodied victims of the cataclysm at Pompeii. Brancusi had also turned away from Rodin, and, for a brief moment in 1909 and 1910,

2

3, 5   Archipenko was carving figures (WOMAN, HEAD ON KNEE; WOMAN WITH CAT) that stayed monumentally close to the shape of the block. The archetype in this kind is perhaps Brancusi's THE KISS of 1908. In Archipenko, however, there are already conflicting planes building up a tension in the form, and the sculptor's instinct for the swelling curve was to offset this blockiness.

7   The fluid yet massive little figure, REPOSE (1911)—seen at the
10   Armory Show along with his FAMILY LIFE—hints at the elegance to come. We have already passed the architecturally inspired SILHOUETTE, a completely accomplished and nearly abstract spiral
9   figure of 1910. MADONNA OF THE ROCKS is curvilinear Cubism before its time, and a similar composition that goes a long step
8   further into the abstract is DRAPED WOMAN, an up-piling into a pyramid of swirling form. And then we come to
6   the altogether exceptional PENCHÉ.

This little leaning figure sets a life pattern for Archipenko. The image is impersonal, the bulk is gone, and a series of tubular forms or cones with an oval, featureless head provide the plastic vocabulary. In its smoothness it has a "streamlined" quality, although the word had yet to come into existence; and here is the mannerist *objet d'art* aspect that criticism was quick to assign to Archipenko and has been slow to see in Brancusi. But PENCHÉ is essentially construction with an implied inner backbone or armature that gives it subtle strength. The only things lacking are the Archipenko concaves and voids. He had yet to slice into the cylinder and show us the forms from the inside. In retrospect,

23. Woman with Fan (1914) 35¾″

PENCHÉ seems so essential to Archipenko's life work that we ask whence it could have come.

Among his many sources, Archipenko himself lists Byzantine art. There is reference to images in the cathedral of St. Sophia at Kiev. The elongated figure that is Archipenko's own, is she not essentially Byzantine? Is not the characteristic oval head her Byzantine head from now on and her drapery which is part of her physical and spiritual anatomy, in its series of planes and cones (oftentimes later ribbed or grained), the very essence of Byzantine drapery?

Archipenko is full of language that describes Byzantine art. "All ideas exist forever in the universe at all times, in earth, air, and water, and simultaneously belong to all that exists, has existed or may exist in future, and may serve any purpose." Or, "a perfect example of spiritual detachment from material existence is music," or "through the modulation of space, our consciousness participates in the creative process because that which does not exist is re-created within us in the abstract form of space, and becomes a reality in our optical memory . . . For me the non-existence of something known provoked the desire and impulse to transform the absent into reality." Archipenko liked to quote Bergson who perhaps led him into the incongruity of a lifetime which troubled neither Bergson nor Archipenko—the drive to be at once dynamic and timeless. Archipenko uses the word "dynamic" constantly. And flux and flow may have challenged the basic Byzantine armature of his art. But contradictions do no harm to an artist; they provide tension.

31. Española (Head and Still Life) (1916) 21″ x 23″

This stressing of a Byzantine source is not offered out of the vanity of interpretation, for if Archipenko is a maker of icons, does it not account for decades of design adjustment and refinement in several of his major images? Is not ritual art an endless approach to invisible conception? Brancusi's life work followed the same pattern: invention, refinement, elimination, repetition. Archipenko delighted in the translation of forms into different media; they reappear like a creed in different languages.

In the two years before the First World War, we come to major achievements. To quote Alfred H. Barr, Jr. (*Cubism and Abstract Art*, 1936): "Archipenko, who had studied Egyptian and archaic Greek figures in the Louvre after his arrival in Paris in 1908, was the first to work seriously and consistently at the problem of Cubist sculpture. . . . After a series of solid Cubistic figures Archipenko modeled in 1912 the radically original WALKING WOMAN in which the Cubist search for far-fetched analogies in the deformation of 'nature' is applied to sculpture by substituting voids for solids in the face and torso and concavities and convexities in the left leg and the skirt.The figure was tinted in two tones, perhaps the first departure toward the polychrome which became so conspicuous in Cubist sculpture and construction of 1915-20.

"In 1912 Archipenko also made the first of his famous MEDRANO series of figure constructions in polychrome glass, wood and metal."

Archipenko's voids for solids and concavities for convexities are by no means arbitrary devices. In hollowing the figure, he subjects it to more complete exposure than it had ever sustained

Russian caricature, 1915.
Archipenko's work used as the
caricature of Wilhelm II

11

before. The figure lies open to us, and we are aware of it from the inside as it is aware of itself. His new momentous discovery and mastery of living voids, with a matrix or shell enclosing them, states clearly that we are a sentient illusion, hollows within hollows, and voids within voids, and that the inner core or personality is the most immaterial part of us.

At this pre-war date begins the use of color, whether in the construction to which Barr refers, or in painted plaster and terra cotta. We see it in this exhibition only in some subdued degree, as color went over into the bronzes. Archipenko did not invent polychrome sculpture, but he used color in sculpture as it had never been used before, and it was to grow upon him—his later work is increasingly polychromatic. For Archipenko, color sets off that division between inner core and outer shell·which is so important to him. Just as his concavities give him a whole new range in composition, with a new system of shadows, so color allows Archipenko to superimpose form on form.

Previously, color in sculpture had served to simplify; it went over sculpture like costume, and costume, with its symbolism, was often reason enough for its introduction. But in the real world, color and form are frequently at cross purposes. Color is often for camouflage, for creating an image which does not exist. So it is with the coloration of birds and reptiles. If we bear this in mind, we can see how the sculptor makes form and color impinge on each other, sometimes to reinforce each other, sometimes for the tension between them. This is using color in an essentially modern

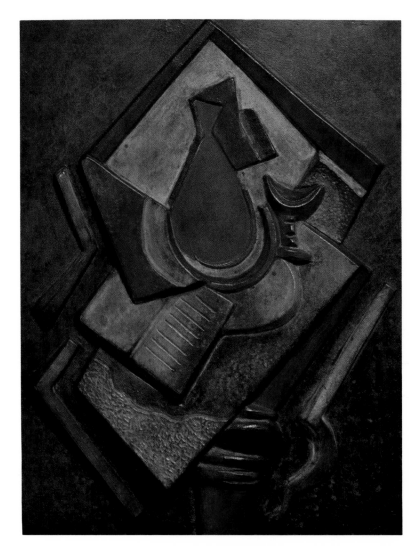

34. Still Life with Book and Vase on the Table (Still Life) (1918) 18″ x 13¾″

way, for controlled complexity. But color patterns fused into sculpture have once more become a common experience; there is no need to argue their case.

12 1912 saw DANCE, two fragmentary figures that join hands to define an open space that becomes the core and unity of the

14 composition, and this work leads on to the BLUE DANCER (1913), a lyric, airy creature. The shape of spaces is as carefully studied here as are the solid forms. This sculpture breathes the spirit of an epoch, but Archipenko can do still better, and step out of his time,

17 as with GREEN CONCAVE of the same year. Here he achieves forms that appear altogether noble and primeval. The relation between hollow torso and solid limb strikes us as profound truth; so does the single raised arm, or enough of arm to determine a gesture, and the raised arm reveals a breast. On the other side there is nothing; no gesture, hence no arm, hence no breast. Then (we are still in 1913) come the pure intersecting planes of the

15 construction, HEAD, possibly his most successful Cubist work, a complete transformation into geometric terms and negative space without loss, even of personality.

Archipenko was given an exhibition in Berlin by Herwarth Walden in 1913. At the time, Apollinaire wrote on Archipenko in Walden's *Der Sturm*: "One senses in the solemn character of Archipenko's art a religious influence in the development of his temperament. Holy, naive pictures must have been a delight for his eyes as a child." Apollinaire must have thought well of his exuberant essay, as he parsimoniously re-worked it in his

36. Standing Woman (1920) 28½″ x 16⅜″

comments on the Salon des Independents of February, 1914.

In this same fateful year, Archipenko produced what Barr

22 considers his finest sculpture: BOXERS, a work that has to be mentioned in any history of twentieth-century art. Here we have an architectonic cage of thrust and counter-thrust that makes a

12 composition of the space it encloses, as did DANCE before it. Also of

21 this same year is GONDOLIER, a superb silhouette, completely stylized, and all the more communicative. The man's sweep merges with a leg, and all is managed with the dignified adroitness

24 of a gondolier at work. GEOMETRIC STATUETTE, also of this year, is a perfect little image, at once "minimal" and bold in conception.

19 The sharp-edged, blade-like FLAT TORSO (1914) is followed two

30 years later by WHITE TORSO, which introduces the neoclassical

27 Archipenko. WOMAN COMBING HER HAIR (1915) is one of his most renowned sculptures, very simple (granted the complexities that are now Archipenko's special contributions), monumental, and quite goddess-like in her detachment.

Archipenko lived in Nice for the duration of the war.

31 Important works came out of those years. ESPAÑOLA (1916) is a relief that is both figure and still life on table, an imagery that one

29 might expect to see reserved for painting. SEATED BLACK CONCAVE

17 (1916) carries the composition of GREEN CONCAVE (1913) further.

33 EGYPTIAN MOTIF (1917) testifies by form and title to Archipenko's early concern with Egyptian sculpture—the svelte forms, the tapered body resolved into geometry, the dignity, the simplification, all this spoke to him. It is a motif that will recur

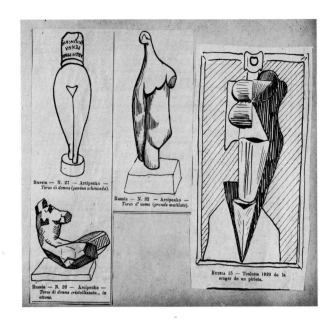

Italian caricatures of Archipenko's works in connection with the exhibition of his sculptures at the Venice Biennale, 1920

with and without color, for in his use of color there is a debt to
Egypt too. The inverted cone from the knee down, as we see it in
this sculpture, has become part of Archipenko's language. He is a
very conscious, inventive artist. Perhaps—and here he was ahead
of his time (our time) for better or worse—he was completely
committed to aesthetic inventiveness. For instance, in this figure,
one breast, concave, is the inversion of the other. One must accept
that in Archipenko the emotion is integral to the idea.

There is a "sculpto-painting" in the next year, a relief well over
on the side of painting, but heightened into actuality. STILL LIFE
34 WITH BOOK AND VASE ON THE TABLE is rich in color that translates
31 well into bronze, only less arresting than the ESPAÑOLA relief
of two years before.

In 1918 Archipenko modeled VASE FIGURE (RAY is its variant).
Earlier than Brancusi's BIRD IN SPACE, it inevitably invites
35 comparison with it. RAY does not celebrate flight, but the amazing
erectness of the human body. There is just enough modulation
to make plain that it is a figure; it stands with serenity and poise,
and the half moon that serves for head (the oval of face outlined)
is alert and lovely. RAY has all the Archipenko virtues, and an
overriding dignity achieved without the price of heaviness.
37 In GEOMETRIC FIGURE WITH SPACE AND CONCAVE (1920), a
seated figure, the excitement comes definitely from the abstract
quality, for the observer as it does for the artist, and there is
a sense of upward climbing, of elevation, of verticality as a
characteristic achievement. One feels that he cannot take this

4. Black Seated Torso (1909) 15″

development further without breaking the figure into fragments, or else bringing it support, and these are precisely the steps

36 he takes. The verticality of STANDING WOMAN (1920) is achieved by the symmetrically placed curvilinear elements that rise out of the receding blue bronze. By contrast, Archipenko then modeled a

38 large figure, TURNING TORSO (1921), using the Hellenic half turning torso as a point of departure. But then the deliberate takes over, and the turn becomes tighter, the waist narrower, the axis more defined.

The first years after the war were a time of travel. Archipenko was given a one-man show at the Venice Biennale in 1920. He married Angelica Schmitz in 1921 and for the next two years lived in Berlin. Here he opened a school—he had had a school in Paris as early as 1912, and he would always continue to teach. From Berlin he came to America. He seems to have had a willingness to burn bridges, yet his staying in the United States was more expedience than pilgrimage; he originally planned to exhibit in Japan, with America as a stopover. Wherever he went in America he taught: in New York, in Seattle, in Los Angeles, and for a long time in Chicago, then back in New York and in Woodstock.

His first decade in America included a period of graceful attenuated naturalism—perhaps in an effort to be in contact with the world around him. There is a certain amount of dashing portraiture; many times the model is his new wife. Of a number of

41 little deities, perhaps the best is MELANCHOLY (1931). It is really

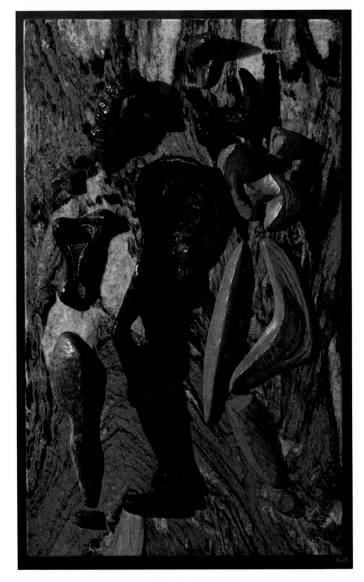

61. Fragmentary Relief (1959) 23″ x 14″

quite grand, in its Baroque way, with the excitement of large concept in small scale. Photography can bring out this largeness. Archipenko's sculpture photographs well, for that matter, being a strongly defined and conceptual art. Its refinement discourages touching, which would break the spell of its presence. It has the excitement of ideas, the low temperature of thought.

42   TORSO IN SPACE, 1935 and 1936, exists in many versions, one life-size. The svelte, reclining, upward bent figure has a Madame Recamier to Pauline Bonaparte pose, and indeed, mood; we are uncomfortably in the presence of elegance, and are reminded that elegance, in this century at least, is a packaged product.

19   TORSO IN SPACE belongs to the family of FLAT TORSO and
30   WHITE TORSO, and one suspects that in that moment of very hard times for him and others, in the 1930's, this was the sculpture that most people managed to like most easily, for it became unfairly
55   a symbol of the artist. LYING HORIZONTAL FIGURE (1957) is one of the last of these streamlined female silhouettes, brought to an abstract conclusion.

43   Then in 1936, SEATED BLACK comes as a culmination of the familiar seated torso image. It has a poised strength and simplicity in place of the more open and articulated qualities.

44   In ARCHITECTURAL FIGURE (1937), one is tempted to see the first of a new phase. Actually, it is only a revival of vivid polychrome, but it is a magical event, colored like a Japanese pheasant. And where was the audience for this in the mid-thirties? We were illustrating poverty.

62. Kimono (1961) 31½″

In the mid-forties, Archipenko produced sculptures in plastic into which he fed light from below, so that they glow with inner-lighted perimeters, like events in space. The light is thus completely controlled, in fact it is the controlling of light that is the sculpture. As always, these plastics are perfect performances. With Archipenko there never seems to be any evident technical groping; he is a superb craftsman, here exploring methods of

45 carving plastic with complex machinery. Seated figure (1947) is typical of Archipenko's rising forms translated into this new

46 medium, religious motif (1948) of his frontal hieratic figures. Much was made of these inventions when his work was shown in Europe again in 1955-56. One has the feeling, however, that this is only one more phase of a mobilization of resources, a preparation for the new.

For Archipenko does achieve his final breakthrough in his last ten years; it is quite true that his two periods of greatest inventiveness are the first and last decades of his life as an artist. One must see his late objects in relation to the times that have come upon us. A willingness to use all materials, any method, now has general acceptance. It is now a moment when an exceptional idea is demanded, together with exceptional technical control; there must be no fumble. But often these requirements are not by any means fused, often idea and performance are invited to

52 glare forth as ends in themselves. Multi-colored figure (1957) is such a work. The interest vacillates between form-color and hard opaque surface. A figure composed of separate elongated

Cleopatra (1957) wood, bakelite, polychrome 38″ x 84″

26

fragments rises from a background as though breaking the surface of a bath. The rest is a womb-like surround in various levels and colors—Archipenko's typical oval containing walls. The sculptor does not bother to remind us of anything in our experience, unless we share the experience of his previous work. It is MEDRANO II (a revolutionary painted construction using multi-materials, in the Guggenheim Museum, New York) up to date, with the emphasis on the magical and the forms now taken for granted.

50   In OVAL FIGURE of much the same moment, the shape of the figure is a vacancy; the concrete object, light in tone, and fat in full relief, is the space around the figure materialized. The substances are bone clean and smooth. By now, bakelite, mirror background and glass hard surfaces demand an industrial designer's sensibility. The surfaces are easy to resent. These objects raise distracting questions and unsettle definitions. Before they carry conviction, they mar earlier pleasures, until one says: Let us be fair, the past is past. The sculptor is ahead of his time.

    The extreme event of this productive year, 1957, is CLEOPATRA.
52 This is an Arabian Nights fantasy beside which MULTI-COLORED FIGURE is pale and dim. The gold and ivory body is its own couch or barque. Somewhere there is blue sea and a shimmer of wood grain, like water or watered silk. A swan neck, that doubles for an arm, reaches forward and upward, without head, but with a small Egyptian eye, and looks at itself in a real mirror. The reflection is unescapably there, to confirm the hallucination.

47. Medieval (1953) 25″ x 21″

A real silver bracelet, a real handful of coral beads, and crystalline stone appear in the background, like objects put into evidence. This is something that an ancient mariner, magically drawing on all the resources of art, might have carved out of whale ivory at the end of a long voyage. Before such an hypnotic presence, who can talk of planes and textures and such jargon? What is important is to avoid the mirror. If symbols are to work, they must be new, and genius is never embarrassed. Archipenko has, in CLEOPATRA, marshalled a life's experience in use of convex, concave, reflection, floating forms, "sculpto-painting" and assemblage.

Decidedly the sculpture has come alive in a new way. Form is no longer an end in itself; it exists for the magic it contains—

62 to hypnotize. This quality is now inherent. In KIMONO (1961), Archipenko has taken the voids usually located at the heads of his statues and opened the main trunk of the torso. The psyche thus emanates through a "heart" rather than through the cerebral center. This shift is reinforced by a fascinating double image— these voids that are breasts also become eyes in a mask-like shape.

65 FESTIVE (1961) is a *tour de force* of texture and polychrome even more provocative than KIMONO. In this cloaked figure the front view is unabashedly exposed, while from the rear the all-encompassing garment becomes a formidable enclosure. The dichotomy between exposure and inaccessibility reinforced by the polychrome, stirs the fantasies normally allocated to the theatre; the detachment associated with sculpture has vanished.

65. Festive (1961) 26½″

28

At this late hour, Archipenko created a great sculpture,

64 QUEEN OF SHEBA (1961). SHEBA is too complex to dismiss with generalities. Starting with the bottom of this large statue (for it does grow upwards in an evolutionary process), a massive concavity, his largest concave, forms the first structure, heavy through size, but freed of bulk by its flowing surge. Inscribed on the hollow walls is a repeated pattern. Out of the space formed by this enclosure rises a vertical shaft with incised upward parallel lines that moves to the next elevation, a massive disk, which it proceeds to penetrate. The surface of this floor is also incised with concentric patterns. The core tapers, then flares out to support the third and last formal level, a half sphere, its flat and smooth side tilted upwards, reflecting. The second and third tiers are connected by four curved struts. At first glance, one thinks these help support the third level alone but, like a suspension bridge, the second, cantilevered level, is partly supported by these ribs. In addition, a second spatial environment is created by this system. The core now passes through the third tier, emerging in a sculptural shape which can only be interpreted as a symbol of an intelligence. But such detailed visual investigation of SHEBA in no way accounts for the strange imperious sense of the aloof yet alert which invests the figure and gives it its unity.

66 WOMAN IN THE CHAIR (1963) is somehow related to the QUEEN OF SHEBA. She sits regal, yet strangely benevolent, the magic of the earlier piece remaining in the one gimlet eye.

67 Archipenko's KING SOLOMON (1963) is horned like Moses, spiky,

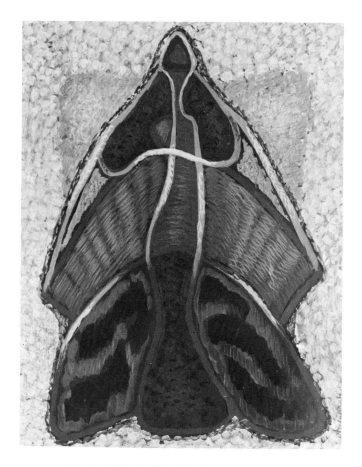

91. Festive (1961) 27½″ x 21½″

august. One must remind oneself when viewing this small sculpture that its architectonics—Archipenko has fused his Cubist and organic shapes into symbolic architecture—were designed for monumental scale, sixty feet high. The idea of this colossus, seen with its diagonal shafts reflecting the atmosphere as no ancient colossus could, is, perhaps, for the artist's last sculpture, his most fitting legacy.

His late images have a quality which cannot be rationally explained; they are unified by a presence within them which does not seem to be directly related to their form or shape. But we recognize them, and they us, and this recognition has a vaguely ennobling effect on the beholder. It is as though Archipenko, in his early work, was able to make plain that a void was there, and in his last work was able to fill it.

But then there are the drawings and prints, and, above all, the remarkable sculpture studies from 1932-35. When so little seemed to be happening, we can look at sculptures that had yet to come into being, and did in due course. Here Archipenko explains himself: shells, carapaces, endlessly the sense of hidden core, of contrast between opaque outside, and the transparent living void, a world in which the appearance versus the inner reality of woman is an endless theme. Archipenko's art is to make a division between sacred and profane space.

FREDERICK S. WIGHT

30

Archipenko's drawings and prints fall into two general categories: those which are studies for sculpture and those which use existent sculpture as a point of departure for further research. The sketches of 1932 to 1935, for example, were eventually realized in sculpture, were rejected, or further refined in subsequent drawings. The closeness of the sketch to the final sculpture is striking—simplicity and self-assurance are so evident that we might well interpret them as the final conception before working in the round. However, by observing the artist's notations on concaves, space, textures and colors, we can follow his continuing creative process of choice and refinement. Those which were selected for sculpture and those rejected, taken together, give us an *entrée* into the sculptor's symbolic language.

91 The color drawing, FESTIVE (1961), which evolved from a small work sketch, is the artist's color and textural research for the polychromed bronze of the same name. Although the color in the drawing is more vivid than in the sculpture, the balance and interaction of textures, colors, volumes, and silhouette are basically established. The translation into bronze is not facile, since the sculpture has its own color-patina requirements and adjustments, problems inherent in bronze polychromy.

80
45 The drawing, SPACE, LIGHT, TRANSPARENCY (1948), was done after the plexiglass sculpture, SEATED FIGURE (1947). The carved plastic's internal lighting could only be studied after it existed sculpturally and could be lit; Archipenko probably believed that by carefully drawing this phenomenon *post facto* he could explore sculpted light for further work in a technique

116. Luminosité des Formes (1963) 30″ x 22″

he was pioneering. It is interesting to compare this drawing with his use of luminosity in LES FORMES ENCERCLÉES (1963), from the St. Gallen series, where a bent light effect has been masterfully achieved with the lithographic crayon. Other drawings

83   concerned with internal light include PEOPLE (c. 1951) and

79   ILLUMINATED FIGURES (1948). The former gives cursory indications of where the light would emerge compositionally within the large plexiglass wall. In the latter, the artist used a technique he called "engraved painting." He scratched through an overlay of dark tone to reach a white base, controlling the modeling in this manner and achieving an effect of pure form and intense luminosity. The surrounding vibrant colors add to the electric intensity of this composition.

107   TORSO IN SPACE (1953), the print inspired by the sculpture of the same name of 1935, combines lithography, silk screen and embossing. Archipenko placed the silhouetted form against a pointillist background and silk-screened over a reflecting aluminum ink, to produce an over-all vibration that offsets the serene and self-contained torso. He has also placed in the upper right of the print a figure which subtly emerges from the background, thus creating the familiar classical dialogue. The contour of the torso in space has been further accented by embossing its silhouette. This major print in Archipenko's graphic *oeuvre* hints at sculptural concepts to come, namely CLEOPATRA (1957). The imagery is prepared and its intrinsic arrangement with mixed media is indicated.

106   The lithograph, COQUETTE (c. 1950), is superficially reminiscent

of the style of Marie Laurencin. But the deep sculptural form of this figure has an almost ominous presence and explores the thematic material expanded upon in Archipenko's late 66 sculpture, such as WOMAN IN THE CHAIR (1963) or even 64 QUEEN OF SHEBA (1961). The dark blue of this lithograph, a pigment first applied to his early German lithographs, heightens the perception of form in space—a patina device he occasionally 63 used in his late sculpture, such as LINEAR ORIENTAL (1961). Archipenko produced many lithographs during his residence in Germany between 1920 and 1923. The number is unclear, for there is yet to be prepared a *catalogue raisonné* of the artist's graphic works, but it is known that they had a broad influence on artists in Western Europe and even in Poland. One of these 102 prints is TWO WOMEN (1921), from the important collaborative portfolio, *Die Bauhaus Mappen*. The soft lithographic strokes 104 and open composition of STILL LIFE (1922) contrast with other artists' cubist prints of this subject which were usually etched. It is interesting to compare this print with the "sculpto-painting," STILL LIFE (1957), and its bronze counterpart of the same year.

Realizing a sculpture from a drawing sometimes involved a time gap as wide as a half a century. One example is the small 98 lithograph, SEATED FIGURE (1913), his earliest known print, 60 from which the bronze relief, ABSTRACTION, was made in 1959.

103 The little drypoint, ANGELICA (1922), is also in the Cubist mode, with its deep angular strokes. Here again, as in his two delicate 101 100 drypoints, KNEELING, and BENDING (1916), Archipenko is working out sculptural problems. The head of ANGELICA is to

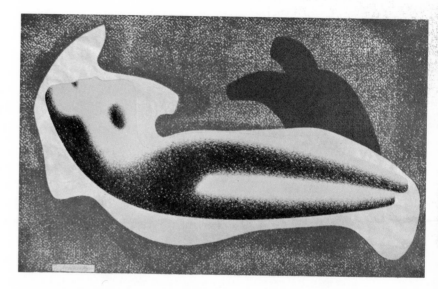

107. Torso in Space (1953) 14⅞″ x 23¾″

appear in this three-quarter view in terra cotta and bronze, merged into a solid background.

109, 118 The series of ten lithographs entitled LES FORMES VIVANTES (1963), his last prints, also evolved from the type of pencil notations alluded to earlier. Each one can be interpreted as a projected sculptural problem expressed planographically. They range from concentrated volume to expanding space, from controlled atmospheric rendering to sfumato, from chiaroscuro to calligraphy. The lithographic medium is exploited in all its gradations and vibrant contrasts. The white of the paper functions in many ways: as a color, as an internal or spatial light or as a subtle highlight. There is an audacity in Archipenko's use of this medium which takes getting used to. As our vision clears, the cogency of the title, LES FORMES VIVANTES, becomes revealed; these are truly living forms that can provoke the viewer and draw him into creative participation. The large lithographs were more than studies for individual sculptures, they were massive stimuli. Unfortunately, they were produced at the end of the artist's long career (he was seventy-four) with no time left to finish the sculptural journey that they chart.

When evaluating the spectrum of Archipenko's work on paper, his sketches, studies, gouaches, pastels and collages, and his etchings and lithographs, one is inclined to rank him as one of the most versatile and acute draftsmen among the master sculptors of this century.

DONALD H. KARSHAN

SCULPTURE

1. Adam and Eve (1908) 19¾″

2. Crossed Arms (1908) 13⅛″

9. Madonna of the Rocks
(La Mere dans les Roches) (1912) 20¼″

5. Woman with Cat (1910) 13¼″

3. Woman (Head on Knee) (1909) 17″

8. Draped Woman (1911) 22″

7. Repose (1911) 13½″ x 14½″

6. Penché (Bending) (1910) 11⅝″

11. Walking (1912) 52½″

10. Family Life (1912) 22″

13. Seated Figure (1912) 15½″

14. Blue Dancer (1913) 41″

12. Dance (1912) 24⅛″ x 19″

60. Abstraction (1959) 17″ x 17″

98. Seated Figure
lithograph
(1913) 11¼″ x 8⅞″

22. Boxers (Struggle) (1914) 23½″ x 18″

17. Green Concave (Woman
Combing Her Hair) (1913) 19⅛″

16. Seated Geometric Figure
(Seated Figure) (1913) 18″

18. Small Reclining Figure (1913) 4⅛″ x 12⅛″

19. Flat Torso (1914) 15¼″

21. Gondolier (1914) 32½″

24. Geometric Statuette (Statuette) (1914) 27″

26. Seated Woman
Combing Her Hair (1915) 21⅛″

20. Statue on Triangular Base
(Statuette) (1914) 29⅞″

27. Woman Combing Her Hair
(1915) 71″

28. Portuguese (Woman Standing) (1916) 24"

29. Seated Black Concave
(Seated Figure) (1916) 30½"

35. Ray (1919) 63¼"

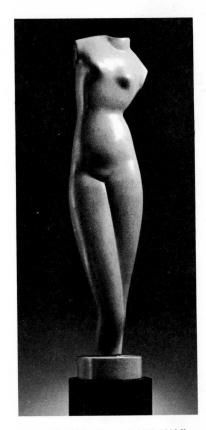

30. White Torso (1916) 18¾"

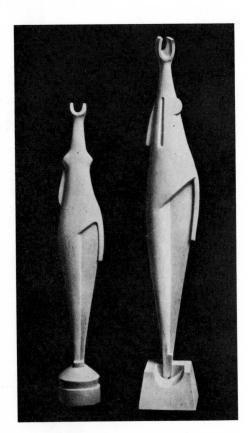

Left: Vase Figure (1918) 18"
Right: Vase Figure (1919) 23"
(Source for Ray)

33. Egyptian Motif (1917) 13¾″

37. Geometric Figure with Space and Concave
(Geometric Seated Figure) (1920) 25½″

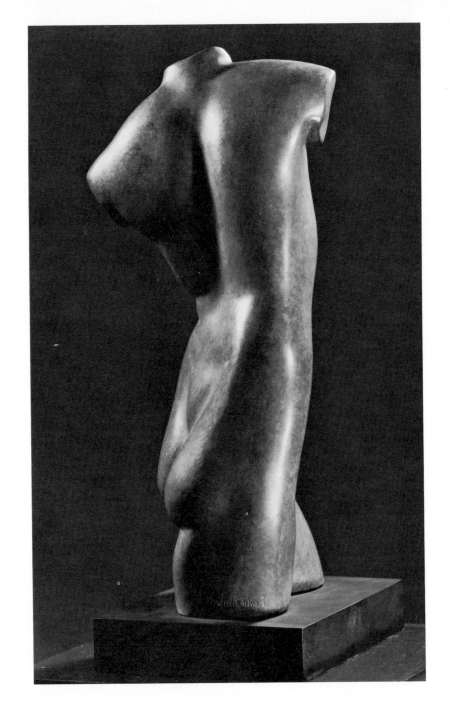

38. Turning Torso (1921) 28"

41. Melancholy (1931) 13¾″

40. Hand (c.1928) 7″

43. Seated, Black (1936) 21⅛″

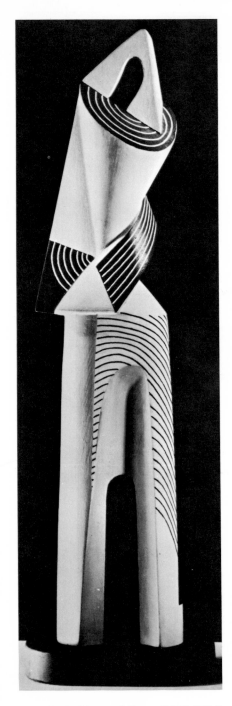

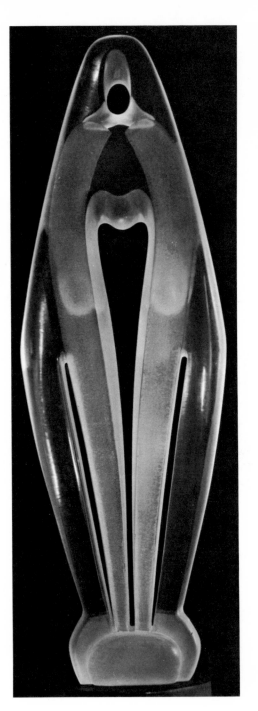

44. Architectural Figure (1937) 34⅜″
(wood, polychromed)

45. Seated Figure (1947) 22½″
(carved plastic)

46. Religious Motif (1948) 36″
(carved plastic)

48. Dualism (1954) 22⅜″

50. Oval Figure (1957) 43″ x 36½″
(wood, bakelite)

53. Orange and Black (1957) 49″ x 25″
(wood, metal, bakelite)

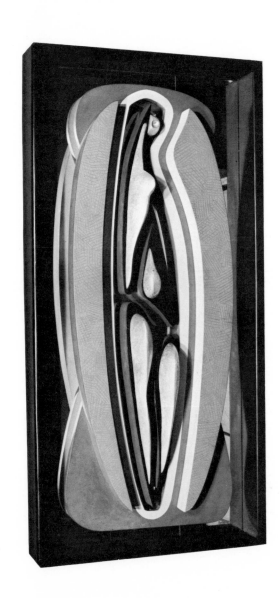

52. Multi-colored Figure (1957) 51¾″ x 25¾″
(wood, metal, plastic)

54. Walking (1957) 16½″

58. Flying (1957) 11½″

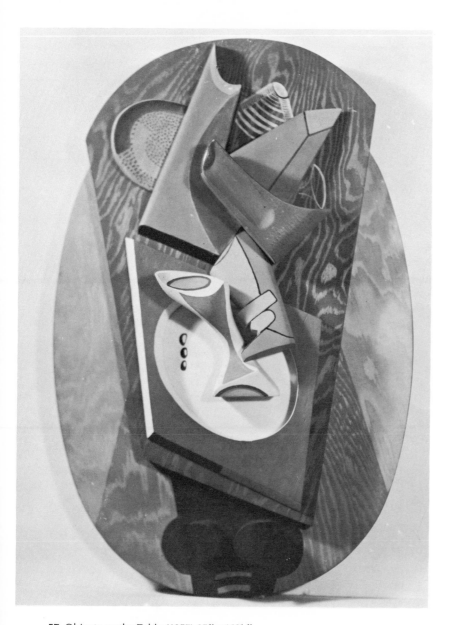

57. Objects on the Table (1957) 25″ x 16¾″

55. Lying Horizontal Figure (Lying Figure) (1957) 5½″ x 14″

63. Linear Oriental (1961) 24½″

64. Queen of Sheba (1961) 65″

66. Woman in the Chair (Seated Woman) (1963) 11⅝″

67. King Solomon (1963) 26¼″

DRAWINGS

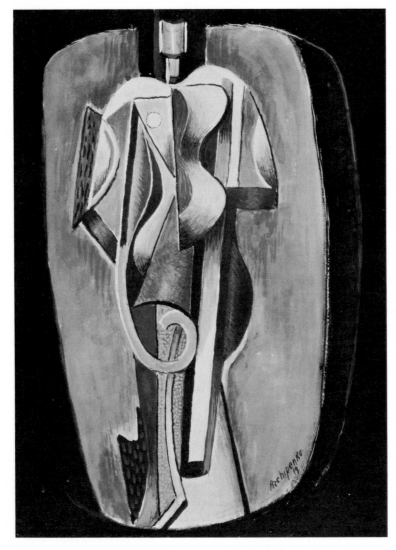

70. Figure, sketch for sculpto-painting (1919) 13⅝″ x 9¾″

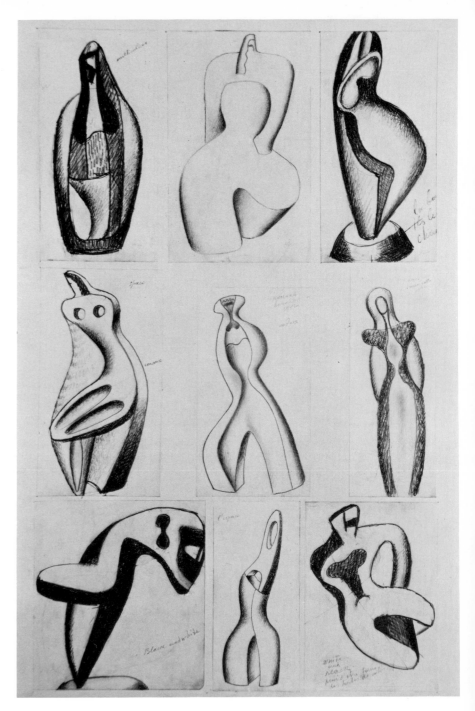

72. Nine Work Sketches for Sculpture (1932-1935) 29¼″ x 18⅝″

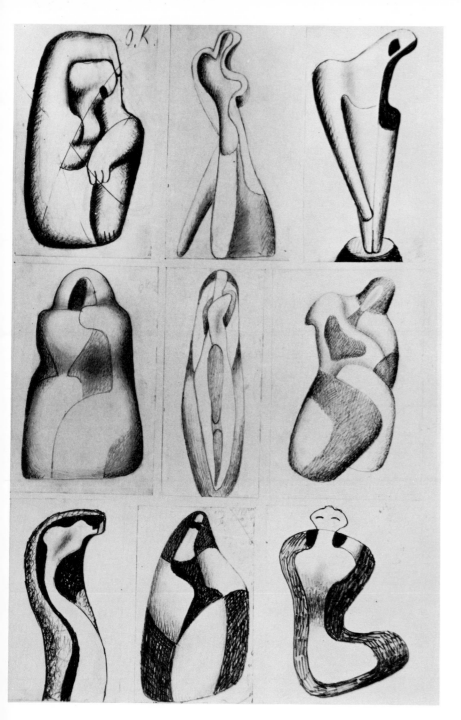

73. Nine Work Sketches for Sculpture (1932-1935) 29½″ x 18¾″

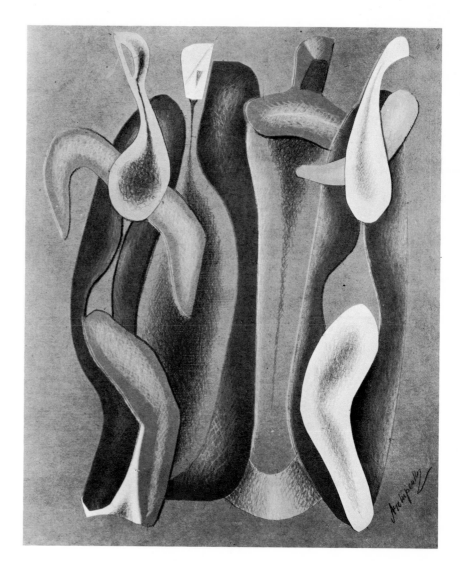

92. Four Figures (1962) 13¾″ x 11¼″

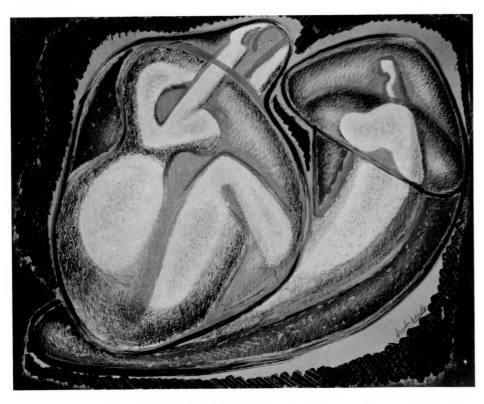

89. Two Figures (1960) 21½″ x 27½″

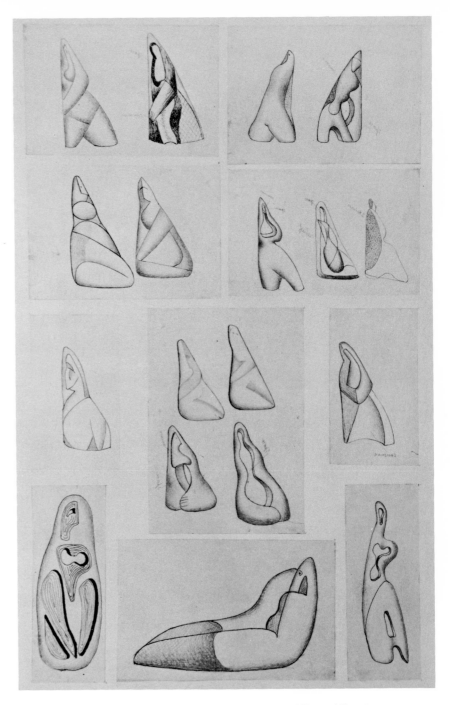

75. Ten Work Sketches for Sculpture (1932-1935) 28½″ x 17¾″

93. Linear Ovals (1962) 27⅝″ x 21½″

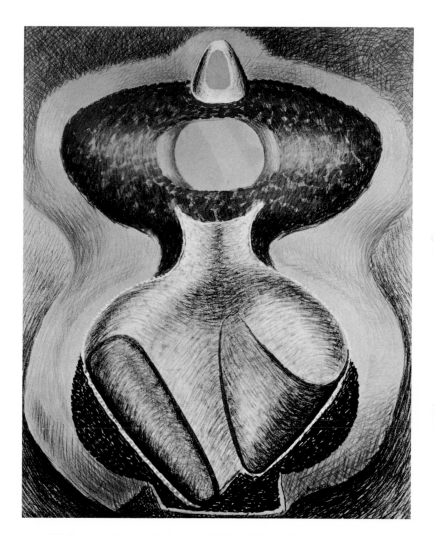

94. Figure on Orange Background (1962) 31¾″ x 26¼″

PRINTS

104. Still Life (1922) 12″ x 16″

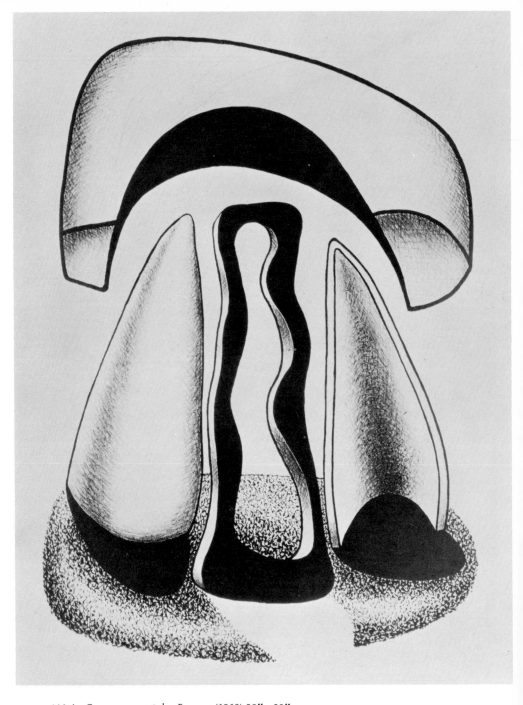

114. Le Couronnement des Formes (1963) 30″ x 22″

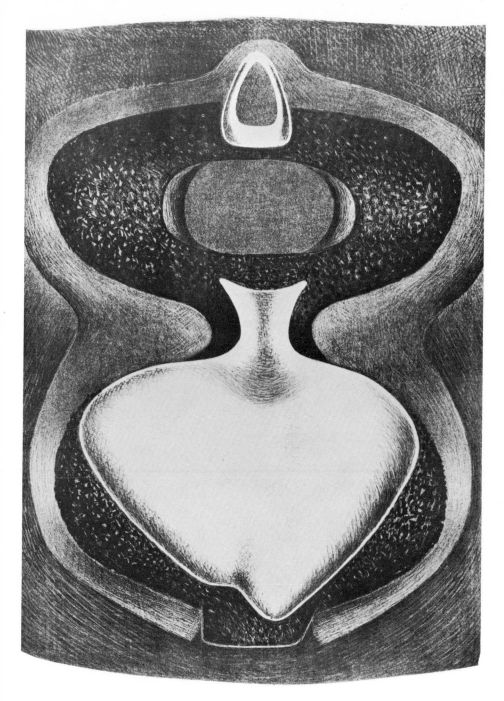

117. Les Formes Majestueuses (1963) 30″ x 22″

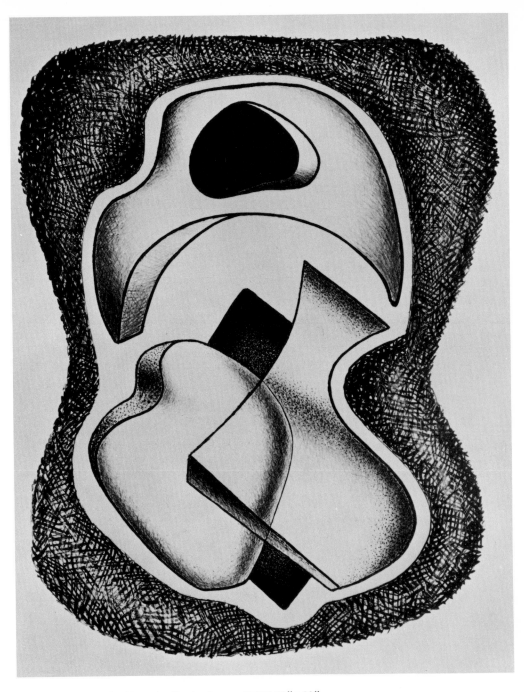

118. Les Rendez-Vous des Quatre Formes (1963) 30″ x 22″

CATALOGUE

When Archipenko produced a variant design based on an earlier idea that he had previously developed, he dated the new variant with the early source date. There are sixteen sculptures in the exhibition (those with asterisks in the listing below) that were produced during an approximate ten year period from 1950 through 1960, in which the artist worked from several early designs and refined and modified them. Several of the source designs were first done in papier-mâché and other perishable materials. Others, like the FAMILY LIFE plaster, were destroyed in World War I. By making the later variants, the artist was able to work the older ideas and modify them according to subsequent experiences, as well as to enable the making of permanent bronze editions.

All sculptures are in bronze unless otherwise noted.

Names in parentheses are other titles by which sculptures are or were known. Casts "A" are artist's casts.

Measurements do not include small attached bases designed by the artist. A single dimension refers to height; with more than one dimension, height precedes width.

1. 1908   ADAM AND EVE, 19¾″, cast 1/8.

2. 1908   CROSSED ARMS, 13⅛″, cast 2/12.

3. 1909   WOMAN (HEAD ON KNEE), 17″, cast 3/8.

4. 1909   BLACK SEATED TORSO, 15″, cast "A."

5. 1910   WOMAN WITH CAT, 13¼″, cast 1/12.

6. 1910   PENCHÉ (BENDING), bronze, chromium plated, 11⅝″, cast 2/6.

7. 1911   REPOSE, 13½″ x 14½″, cast 7/8.

8. 1911   DRAPED WOMAN, 22″, cast 4/6.

9. 1912   MADONNA OF THE ROCKS (LA MÈRE DANS LES ROCHES), 20¼″, cast 4/6.

10. 1912   *FAMILY LIFE, 22″, cast 1/12. Cast from plaster circa 1960 which is a variant of the six foot high plaster destroyed in World War I.

11. 1912   *WALKING, polychromed, 52½″, cast "A." Cast from plaster circa 1958 which is a variant of the 24″ plaster conceived in 1912. A 27″ variant was made in 1918 and another was made in 1935.

12. 1912   *DANCE, 24⅛″ x 19″, cast 6/8. Cast from plaster of circa 1955 which is a variant of the plaster conceived in 1912.

13. 1912   SEATED FIGURE, 15½″, cast 1/12.

14. 1913   BLUE DANCER, 41″, cast 8/8.

15. 1913   HEAD, polychromed, 14⅞″, cast 6/6. This cast made from original wood construction of 1913.

16. 1913   *SEATED GEOMETRIC FIGURE (SEATED FIGURE), polychromed, 18″, cast "A." Cast from polychromed terra cotta circa 1935. This is a variant of a plaster conceived in 1913.

17. 1913   *GREEN CONCAVE (WOMAN COMBING HER HAIR), 19⅛″, cast 4/6. Cast from a terra cotta circa 1935 which is a variant of the terra cotta conceived in 1913.

18. 1913   SMALL RECLINING FIGURE, 4⅛″ x 12⅛″, cast 3/12.

19. 1914   FLAT TORSO, 15¼″, cast "A."

20. 1914   *STATUE ON TRIANGULAR BASE (STATUETTE), 29⅞″, cast 5/8. Cast from plaster circa 1955 which is a variant of the plaster conceived in 1914.

21. 1914   *GONDOLIER, 32½″, cast 7/12. Cast from plaster of circa 1955 which is a variant of the plaster conceived in 1914. A 64″ version was made circa 1953.

22. 1914   BOXERS (STRUGGLE), 23½″ x 18″, cast 7/8.

23. 1914   *WOMAN WITH FAN, relief, polychromed, 35¾″, cast 2/8. Cast from plaster circa 1958 which is a variant of painted construction in wood, glass, metal, and canvas conceived in 1914.

24. 1914   *GEOMETRIC STATUETTE (STATUETTE), polychromed, 27″, cast 3/6. Cast from polychromed terra cotta of circa 1935 which is a variant of polychromed terra cotta of 1914.

25. 1915   STATUETTE, 20⅜″, cast 4/6.

26. 1915   SEATED WOMAN COMBING HER HAIR, 21⅛″, cast 4/8.

27. 1915   *WOMAN COMBING HER HAIR, 71″, cast "A." Cast from plaster circa 1952 which is a variant of the 13¾″ plaster conceived in 1915. A 25″ variant was also made.

28. 1916   *PORTUGUESE (WOMAN STANDING), polychromed, 24″, cast 3/6. Cast from a polychromed terra cotta which was produced circa 1935. The terra cotta was based on a monochromed plaster design of 1916.

29. 1916   *SEATED BLACK CONCAVE (SEATED FIGURE), 30½″, cast 5/8. Cast from plaster circa 1958 which is a variant of the 14″ terra cotta conceived in 1916. A 14″ variant was also made.

30. 1916   WHITE TORSO, 18¾″, cast "A."

31. 1916   ESPANOLA (HEAD AND STILL LIFE), relief, polychromed, 21″ x 23″, cast 1/8.

32. 1917   FIGURE, sculpto-painting, oil on canvas and wood, 27″ x 20½″.

33. 1917   EGYPTIAN MOTIF, 13¾″, cast "A."

34. 1918   *STILL LIFE WITH BOOK AND VASE ON THE TABLE (STILL LIFE), relief, polychromed, 13¾″ x 18″, cast 4/8.

Cast from plaster circa 1960, which was based on papier-mâché on wood sculpto-painting of 1918.

35. 1919   *RAY, aluminum, 63¼″, cast 5/6. Cast from plaster of 1956 which is a variant of the 18″ and 23″ plasters conceived in 1918 and 1919 and called "Vase Figures."

36. 1920   *STANDING WOMAN, relief, polychromed, 28½″ x 16⅜″, cast 3/8. Cast from plaster circa 1960, which was based on papier-mâché on wood sculpto-painting of 1920.

37. 1920   *GEOMETRIC FIGURE WITH SPACE AND CONCAVE (GEOMETRIC SEATED FIGURE), 25½″, cast 4/8. Cast from plaster circa 1955 which is a variant of the terra cotta conceived in 1920.

38. 1921   TURNING TORSO, 28″, cast 4/8.

39. 1925   ONWARD (WALKING), bronze, gold plated, 21⅞″, cast 1/8.

40. c.1928   HAND, bronze, gold plated, 7″.

41. 1931   MELANCHOLY, lead, 13¾″, cast 1/3.

42. 1935   TORSO IN SPACE, 8½″ x 27½″.

43. 1936   SEATED, BLACK, 21⅛″, cast 4/6.

44. 1937   ARCHITECTURAL FIGURE, wood, polychromed, 34⅜″.

45. 1947   SEATED FIGURE, carved plastic, illuminated from within, 22½″.

46. 1948   RELIGIOUS MOTIF, carved plastic, illuminated from within, 36″.

47. 1953   MEDIEVAL, relief, polychromed, 25″ x 21″, cast 1/8.

48. 1954   DUALISM, polychromed, 22⅜″, cast 1/8.

49. 1954   QUEEN, wood, polychromed, 34″.

50. 1957   OVAL FIGURE, sculpto-painting, wood, bakelite, 43″ x 36½″.

51. 1957 STATUE ON ALUMINUM BASE (FIGURE), polychromed, 18¼", cast 2/6.

52. 1957 MULTI-COLORED FIGURE, sculpto-painting, wood, metal, plastic, 51¾" x 25¾".

53. 1957 ORANGE AND BLACK, sculpto-painting, wood, metal, bakelite, 49" x 25".

54. 1957 WALKING, polychromed, 16½", cast 1/8.

55. 1957 LYING HORIZONTAL FIGURE (LYING FIGURE), polychromed, 5½" x 14", cast 3/6.

56. 1957 OBJECTS ON THE TABLE, sculpto-painting, wood, 25" x 16¾".

57. 1957 OBJECTS ON THE TABLE, relief, polychromed, 25" x 16¾", cast 1/8. Cast from sculpto-painting, 1957, exhibition catalogue number 56 (above).

58. 1957 FLYING, 11½", cast 3/6.

59. 1959 EAGLE, polychromed bronze on marble, relief, 10½" x 15½", cast number 1/8.

60. 1959 ABSTRACTION, bronze on marble, relief, 17" x 17", cast number 1/6. Based on a design in a lithograph of 1913 (see exhibition catalogue number 98 in prints section).

61. 1959 FRAGMENTARY RELIEF, polychromed bronze on marble, relief, 23" x 14", cast 1/8.

62. 1961 KIMONO, polychromed, 31½", cast 3/8.

63. 1961 LINEAR ORIENTAL, polychromed, 24½", cast 3/8.

64. 1961 QUEEN OF SHEBA, 65", cast 2/8.

65. 1961 FESTIVE, polychromed, 26½", cast 1/8.

66. 1963 WOMAN IN THE CHAIR (SEATED WOMAN), polychromed, 11⅝", cast 3/12.

67. 1963 KING SOLOMON, 26¼", cast 3/12.

DRAWINGS

68. 1911 TWO FIGURES, colored pencil, 18¾" x 11¼". Signed and dated 1911. Drawn in Paris c. 1960 after pencil sketch, "Two Figures" of 1911.

69. 1919 YELLOW-BLUE IN ROSE OVAL, SKETCH FOR CONSTRUCTION, gouache, 13¾" x 9¼". Signed and dated 1919. Drawn c. 1960 after sculpto-painting, "Woman" of 1919.

70. 1919 FIGURE, SKETCH FOR SCULPTO-PAINTING, gouache, 13⅝" x 9¾". Signed and dated 1919. Drawn c. 1960 after sculpto-painting, "Standing Woman" of 1919.

71. c.1932 SEATED NUDE, charcoal and pastel, 20" x 12⅜". Signed.

72. 1932-1935 NINE WORK SKETCHES FOR SCULPTURE, pencil, 29¼" x 18⅝". Signed. Red circles are artist's annotations indicating those that were executed as sculpture.

73. 1932-1935 NINE WORK SKETCHES FOR SCULPTURE, pencil, 29½" x 18¾". Signed. Red circles are artist's annotations indicating those that were executed as sculpture.

74. 1932-1935 FIVE WORK SKETCHES FOR SCULPTURE, pencil, 26¾" x 19⅜". Signed. Red circles are artist's annotations indicating those that were executed as sculpture.

75. 1932-1935 TEN WORK SKETCHES FOR SCULPTURE, pencil, 28½" x 17¾". Signed. Red circles are artist's annotations indicating those that were executed as sculpture.

76. 1932-1935 TEN WORK SKETCHES FOR SCULPTURE, pencil, 26¾" x 21". Signed.

77. 1932-1935 NINE WORK SKETCHES FOR SCULPTURE, pencil, 27¾" x 16½". Signed. Red circles are artist's annotations indicating those that were executed as sculpture.

78. c.1940   MOTHER AND CHILD, pencil, ink and gouache, 17¼" x 11⅜". Signed.

79. 1948   ILLUMINATED FIGURES, oil and ink, 22¾" x 16¾". Signed. The artist engraved lines into the oil paint while still wet, a process he named "engraved painting."

80. 1948   SPACE, LIGHT, TRANSPARENCY, ink and colored pencil, 28⅝" x 14¾". Signed. After lucite sculpture, "Seated Figure," 1947.

81. 1948   AFRICANA, gouache and pencil, 28½" x 7⅜". Signed. After polychromed terra cotta, "Orange and Black," 1940.

82. 1948   THREE FIGURES IN THREE COLORS, ink and colored pencil, 21¾" x 13¼". Signed.

83. c.1951   PEOPLE, pencil and gouache, 10½" x 13". Signed. Study for movable wall in transparent carved plastic, to be illuminated from within.

84. c.1957   STILL LIFE WITH JUG, ink, 18½" x 12¼". Signed.

85. c.1960   STUDY FOR SCULPTO-PAINTING, pencil, 11½" x 7⅞".

86. c.1960   KNEELING FIGURE, pencil. Drawn in Paris. 8⅞" x 6⅝". Signed.

87. 1960   TWO FIGURES, pencil, ink, gouache, 13¼" x 10¾". Signed.

88. 1960   GREY AND WHITE, gouache, 21½" x 13½". Signed and dated 1960.

89. 1960   TWO FIGURES, gouache and pastel, 21½" x 27½". Signed.

90. 1961   SKETCH FOR CONSTRUCTION, gouache, 13¾" x 11⅜". Signed and dated 1961.

91. 1961   FESTIVE, gouache and pastel, 27½" x 21½". Signed. Study for polychromed sculpture, "Festive," 1961.

92. 1962   FOUR FIGURES, collage and colored pencil, 13¾" x 11¼". Signed.

93. 1962   LINEAR OVALS, gouache and colored pencil, 27⅝" x 21½". Signed.

94. 1962   FIGURE ON ORANGE BACKGROUND, gouache and pastel, 31¾" x 26¼". Signed.

95. 1962   STUDY FOR POLYCHROMED WOOD CONSTRUCTION, gouache and pastel, 26⅝" x 32¼". Signed and dated 1962.

96. 1962   THREE FIGURES, gouache and colored pencil, 27½" x 21½". Signed.

PRINTS

97. 1913   TWO FIGURES, lithograph, Paris, 12" x 9". Signed in the stone and annotated by the artist "Lacerba 1914." Reproduced in Lacerba (Italy), 1914.

98. 1913   SEATED FIGURE, lithograph, Paris, 11¼" x 8⅞". Signed and dated in the stone. Reproduced in Lacerba (Italy), 1914. Sculpture relief, "Abstraction," 1959, made after this design.

99. 1916   FIGURE STUDY, lithograph in red, blue, and white on colored paper, Berlin, 19⅛" x 12¼". From the portfolio, "Dreizehn Steinzeichnungen," published by J. W. Zanders, Berlin. Signed in the stone.

100. 1916   BENDING, dry-point etching, 10" x 6". Unsigned. Posthumous proof by Estate of the artist.

101. 1916   KNEELING, dry-point etching, 7" x 5". Signed "A.A." Posthumous proof by Estate of the artist.

102. 1921   TWO WOMEN, lithograph, Berlin, 19" x 12⅞". From the portfolio, "Die Bauhaus Mappen." Signed and dated 1921. Edition of 110.

103. 1922   ANGELICA, dry-point etching, Berlin, 6½″ x 4¼″. Signed and dated 1922.

104. 1922   STILL LIFE, lithograph, Berlin, 12″ x 16″. From the portfolio, "Die Schaffenden." Signed. Edition of 125.

105. 1922   WOMAN, lithograph printed in red, Berlin, 15½″ x 9½″. From the portfolio, "Die Schaffenden." Signed. Edition of 125.

106. c.1950   COQUETTE, lithograph in blue, 13¾″ x 10″. Signed. Artist's proof before signed edition of 150, published by Associated American Artists.

107. 1953   TORSO IN SPACE, lithograph, silk screen, and embossing, 14⅞″ x 23¾″. Artist's proof. Signed.

108. 1962   MOTHER AND CHILD, two-color lithograph, 29⅞″ x 20⅜″. Signed and numbered 48/50. Published by "Im Erker" Press, St. Gallen.

109. 1963   LES AMOUREX, lithograph, 30″ x 22″. Plate #1 of portfolio, "Les Formes Vivantes," published by "Im Erker" Press, St. Gallen. Artist's proof before numbered edition of 75.

110. 1963   LA DANSE NOIRE, lithograph, 30″ x 22″. Plate #2 of portfolio, "Les Formes Vivantes," published by "Im Erker" Press, St. Gallen. Artist's proof before numbered edition of 75.

111. 1963   LE GROUPE, lithograph, 30″ x 22″. Plate #3 of portfolio, "Les Formes Vivantes," published by "Im Erker" Press, St. Gallen. Artist's proof before numbered edition of 75.

112. 1963   LES MANNEQUINS, lithograph, 30″ x 22″. Plate #4 of portfolio, "Les Formes Vivantes," published by "Im Erker" Press, St. Gallen. Artist's proof before numbered edition of 75.

113. 1963   LA FAMILLE D'UNE FORME, lithograph, 30″ x 22″. Plate #5 of portfolio, "Les Formes Vivantes," published by "Im Erker" Press, St. Gallen. Artist's proof before numbered edition of 75.

114. 1963   LE COURONNEMENT DES FORMES, lithograph, 30″ x 22″. Plate #6 of portfolio, "Les Formes Vivantes," published by "Im Erker" Press, St. Gallen. Artist's proof before numbered edition of 75.

115. 1963   LES FORMES ENCERCLÉES, lithograph, 22″ x 30″. Plate #7 of portfolio, "Les Formes Vivantes," published by "Im Erker" Press, St. Gallen. Artist's proof before numbered edition of 75.

116. 1963   LUMINOSITÉ DES FORMES, lithograph, 30″ x 22″. Plate #8 of portfolio, "Les Formes Vivantes," published by "Im Erker" Press, St. Gallen. Artist's proof before numbered edition of 75.

117. 1963   LES FORMES MAJESTUEUSES, lithograph, 30″ x 22″. Plate #9 of portfolio. "Les Formes Vivantes," published by "Im Erker" Press, St. Gallen. Artist's proof numbered edition of 75.

118. 1963   LES RENDEZ-VOUS DES QUATRE FORMES, lithograph, 30″ x 22″. Plate #10 of portfolio, "Les Formes Vivantes," published by "Im Erker" Press, St. Gallen. Artist's proof before numbered edition of 75.

CHRONOLOGY

1887

May 30. Born in Kiev, Ukraine, Russia, to Porfiry Antonovich and Poroskovia Wassilievna Machova Archipenko. Paternal grandfather, icon painter. Father, mechanical engineer and inventor, professor of engineering, University of Kiev.

Privately tutored to age nine, when entered Kiev Gymnasium.

1900

Injured legbone in bicycle accident. Confined to bed age 13-14. Studied and copied Michelangelo drawings from book given to him by grandfather.

1902

Having grasped the relationship between mathematics and art, decided on career in art. Inspired by "the fact that Leonardo's creative genius not only covered art, but science as well as engineering and that he considered mathematics as the foundation of all arts."

Entered art school in Kiev to study painting and then sculpture. Influenced by Byzantine tradition in art, the writings of Andreyev, and later, the revolution of 1905.

1905

Expelled from art school because he criticized his teachers for being "too old fashioned and academic."

1906

First one-man show in a town in the Ukraine.

Went to Moscow, worked and participated in different group shows.

1908

Left for Paris at age 20.

Entered Ecole des Beaux Arts, but left after two weeks, finding the academic system too confining and tedious.

Continued study of art independently in museums. "My real school was the Louvre and I attended it daily." Inspired especially by Egyptian, Assyrian, archaic Greek, and early Gothic works.

Established Montparnasse studio where Modigliani, Gaudier-Brzeska and others studied sculpture with him.

1909

Produced series of revolutionary sculptures, such as SEATED BLACK TORSO, SUZANNE, and WOMAN (HEAD ON KNEE).

1910

Began exhibiting in Salon des Artistes Indépendents (showed in 1910, 1911, 1912, 1913, 1914).

"Section d'Or" formed in Paris. Archipenko among its members, who exhibited together until 1914 and again for a short time after the war. Included Picasso, Braque, Gris, Léger, Delaunay, de La Fresnaye, Villon, Picabia, and Marcel Duchamp.

1911

Exhibited in Salon d'Automne, Paris (also in 1912, 1913, 1919). French newspaper caricatured sculpture, WOMAN WITH CAT, which was displayed in this exhibition.

1912

Opened own art school in Paris.

First one-man exhibition in Germany at Folkwang Museum, Hagen. Catalogue analysis by Guillaume Apollinaire.

Produced sculpture, MEDRANO I (JUGGLER), the first three-dimensional construction in modern sculpture in various painted materials (wood, glass, metal wire). Rejected by jury of Salon d'Automne in Paris; exhibited in Budapest, 1913, in Exposition d'Art Moderne, organized by Alexandre Mercereau.

Started creating reliefs, generally made of plaster, carved and painted, which he named "Sculpto-Peintures." These are the first sculpto-paintings in modern art.

Created WALKING WOMAN, first modern sculpture formed with abstracted concaves to create implied volume and abstracted voids (openings through mass).

Produced DANCE, one of first examples in modern sculpture of creating a spatial environment; reproduced and ridiculed on the cover of the English magazine, *The Sketch*, of October 29, 1913.

1913

Represented by four sculptures and five drawings in Armory Show in New York, including FAMILY LIFE which was ridiculed by caricature in *The World* (New York).

First one-man exhibition at Der Sturm Gallery, Berlin.

Produced highly polychromed sculpture, CARROUSEL PIERROT.

Created HEAD, construction with crossing planes.

1914

Created BOXERS, one of the most abstract modern sculptures done to that date.

Produced GONDOLIER, caricatured in *Le Bonnet Rouge*, No. 16, 7 Mars 1914 (Paris).

Cubist exhibition held by Mánes Society, Prague, organized by Alexandre Mercereau, included five sculptures of Archipenko, five of Brancusi, and six of Duchamp-Villon.

1915

Produced sculpture, WOMAN COMBING HER HAIR, which again used deep concaves and void.

1915-1918

Spent war years working on his sculpture in a villa at Cimiez, a suburb of Nice, loaned him by a wealthy friend.

1918

Produced sculpture, RAY, first of three highly simplified vase figures.

Left collection of plasters of early work with Monsieur and Madame Jean Verdier in Cannes, for safe-keeping, on the eve of his departure for Germany.

1919

Began extensive tour exhibiting his works in various European cities, including Geneva, Zurich, Paris, London, Brussels, Athens, Berlin, Munich, etc., lasting through 1921.

1920

Large one-man show in Biennale Exhibition, Venice (XII Exposizone Internationale d'Arte). Ridiculed in *Telegrafo Livorno* of June 11, 1920. Cardinal La Fontaine, Patriarch of Venice advised the faithful not to attend.

"Section d'Or," of which Archipenko was member, resumed exhibiting after war (in Paris at Gallerie Weill, and in Brussels, 1920; in Rome—organized by Enrico Prampolini, and in Geneva, 1921).

1921

Married Angelica Bruno-Schmitz, German sculptress and great granddaughter of artist, Bonaventura Genelli.

Moved to Berlin, opened own art school.

First one-man exhibition in United States at Société Anonyme, Museum of Modern Art, New York City. Monograph, *Archipenko*, by Ivan Goll (Société Anonyme, 1921) published in connection with this exhibition.

Symposium on the *Psychology of Modern Art and Archipenko* held at Société Anonyme, New York.

Retrospective exhibition in Potsdam. Catalogue introduction by Ivan Goll.

"Archipenko Album" by Ivan Goll, Theodor Däubler and Blaise Cendrars published in Potsdam by Gustav Kiepenheuer Verlag.

One-man exhibition at Der Sturm Gallery, Berlin.

1923

Moved to the United States. Arrived in New York by liner, 'S.S. Mongolia.' Opened art school in New York City.

Professor Hans Hildebrandt's monograph, *Alexander Archipenko*, published in Berlin by Ukrainske Slowo in English, French, German, and Ukrainian (in Spanish by Editora Internacional, Buenos Aires).

Roland Schacht's "Alexander Archipenko," *Sturm Bilderbuch II*, published in Berlin by Verlag Der Sturm.

Prof. Erich Wiese's article, "Alexander Archipenko," *Junge Kunst*, Vol. 40, published in Leipzig by Verlag von Klinkhardt und Biermann.

1924

Opened summer art school in Woodstock, New York.

Invented variable image system as "movable painting" known as "Peinture Changeante" (also called "Archipentura"), (U.S. Patent 1,626,496 granted in 1927), dedicated to Thomas Edison and Albert Einstein. "The observer is shown a screen on which is painted an abstract form. Archipenko presses an electric button, the abstract form begins to change proceeding through most of the phases of the female body Archipenko painted and chiseled."

Featured at one-man exhibition at The Anderson Galleries, New York, in 1928.

1927

One man exhibition, Société des Artistes Nikwa, Tokyo, Japan.

1928

Became an American citizen.

1929

Number of exhibitions of works of students at Arko, a laboratory school for ceramics which Archipenko established in New York City.

Purchased thirteen acres on abandoned rock quarry site near Woodstock, New York, art colony. Began construction of what was to be a complex of art school buildings, his own studio, and new location for his summer art school.

1932

Started to lecture on theories of creativeness in colleges and universities on Pacific Coast, in the Middle West and the East.

1933

Taught at Mills College, Oakland, California (Summer Session), and at Chouinard School, Los Angeles.

1935

Took up residence in California, opened own art school in Los Angeles, and exhibited in several western cities.

1935-1936

Taught summer sessions, University of Washington, Seattle.

1937

Moved to Chicago; opened school of creative fine arts.

Associate instructor at New Bauhaus School of Industrial Arts, Chicago.

1939

Created MOSES, seven foot high sculpture, for benefit of artists exiled by Fascist regimes of Europe, but its planned tour was cancelled due to delays of wartime transportation. During the Nazi purge of "decadent modern art," twenty-two of his paintings and most of his sculpture then owned by German museums were confiscated; and his work was singled out for attack in the Nazi book, *Sauberung des Kunsttempels*, by Wolfgang Willrich (Munich: Verlag J. F. Lehmanns, 1937).

Returned to New York. Re-opened art school as well as summer school in Woodstock, New York.

1944

Taught at the Dalton School, New York.

1946

Taught at the Institute of Design, Chicago.

1947

Produced SEATED FIGURE, the first carved plastic sculpture illuminated from within, featured at his 78th one-man show at the New York Galleries of the Associated American Artists, in 1948.

1950

Taught at the University of Kansas City, Kansas City, Missouri. Commissioned to create two statues for the entrance of the University. The two identical IRON FIGURES, 14-foot high constructions with crossing planes, were completed in 1951.

1950-1951

Made lecture tour of southern cities of United States.

1951

Taught at Carmel Institute of Art, Carmel, California; at the University of Oregon, Eugene, Oregon; and at the University of Washington, Seattle.

1952

Taught at University of Delaware, Newark, Delaware.
Delegate to U.N.E.S.C.O., New York City.
One-man exhibition, Museum of Modern Art, São Paulo, Brazil.

1953

Inaugurated Associate Member of International Institute of Arts and Letters.
One-man exhibition, El Instituto Guatemalteco-Americano, Guatemala City, Guatemala.

1955-1956

Tour of one-man exhibition to six German cities.

1955

Began work on book, *Archipenko: Fifty Creative Years 1908-1958*, by Alexander Archipenko and Fifty Art Historians, a 346 page book which includes a 52 page manifesto on creativity by Archipenko, an extensive bibliography, quotations, and 292 plates of his works.

1956

Taught at the University of British Columbia, Vancouver, Canada.
Produced REVOLVING FIGURE (THE ART OF REFLECTION), a 78-inch high, motorized, revolving construction with crossing planes, made of wood, mother-of-pearl, formica and metal.

1957

Created CLEOPATRA, a 38-inch by 84-inch sculpto-painting of wood and bakelite, polychromed.
December 5. Angelica died at age 65.

1959

Awarded Medaglia D'Oro at XIII Biennale d'Arte Triveneta, III Concorso Internazionale del Bronzetto, Sala della Ragione, Padova, Italy, in October.

1960

Book, *Archipenko: Fifty Creative Years 1908-1958*, by Alexander Archipenko and Fifty Art Historians published by Tekhne Publications, established by Archipenko for the purpose of publishing this book.
August 1. Married Frances Gray, a sculptor and former student.
Recovery of plasters of early works stored in 1918 by Monsieur and Madame Jean Verdier in a gardener's cottage on their property in Cannes.

1961

Produced 66-inch high sculpture, QUEEN OF SHEBA, his last large bronze.

1962

Elected to the Department of Art of the National Institute of Arts and Letters.

1963

Produced LES FORMES VIVANTES, a series of ten lithographs, his last graphics, at Erker-Presse in St. Gallen, Switzerland.
Large retrospective exhibition of Archipenko sculpture, drawings and prints at Ente Premi Roma in Rome and Centro Culturale S. Fedele in Milan in 1963, and at Galerie Stangl in Munich in 1964.

1964

February 25. Alexander Archipenko died in New York, shortly after casting his last sculpture, KING SOLOMON.

1965

Preparations begun for memorial retrospective exhibition sponsored by UCLA and traveling to eleven museums across the country.

SELECTIVE BIBLIOGRAPHY

(A) ARCHIPENKO MONOGRAPHS

Archipenko, Alexander, and Fifty Art Historians, *Archipenko: Fifty Creative Years 1908-1958*. New York: Tekhne, 1960.

Goll, Ivan, "Archipenko," *Horizont*. Vienna, 1921.

Goll, Ivan, *Archipenko: An Appreciation*, translated from the French by Mary Knoblauch. New York: Société Anonyme, Inc., (1921).

Goll, Ivan, Däubler, Theodor and Cendrars, Blaise, *Archipenko Album*. Potsdam: Gustav Kiepenheuer Verlag, 1921.

Golubetz, Nicola, *Archipenko*. Lwow: Ukrainske Mistetstvo, 1922.

Hildebrandt, Prof. Hans, *Alexander Archipenko*. Berlin: Ukrainske Slowo, 1923. (Edition appeared in four languages: English, French, German, Ukrainian.)

Hildebrandt, Prof. Hans, *Alejandro Archipenko*. Buenos Aires: Editora Internacional, 1923. (Spanish edition)

Mitzitch, Lioubomir (ed.), *Archipenko, Plastique Nouvelle*. Belgrade: Editions Zenit, 1923.

Raynal, Maurice, *A. Archipenko, avec 32 reproductions en phototypie*. Rome: "Valori Plastici," 1923.

Schacht, Dr. Roland, *Alexander Archipenko, Sturm-Bilderbuch II*. Berlin: Der Sturm Verlag, 1923.

Wiese, Prof. Erich, "Alexander Archipenko," *Junge Kunst*, Vol. 40. Leipzig: Verlag von Klinkhardt und Biermann, 1923.

(B) BOOKS

Apollinaire, Guillaume, *Chroniques d'Art (1902-1918)*. Textes réunis, avec préface et notes, par L.-C. Breunig. Paris: Gallimard, 1960.

Archipenko, Alexander, "The Extension of Creativity," in Arthur Zaidenberg, *The Art of the Artist: Theories and Techniques of Art by the Artists Themselves*. New York: Crown Publishers, Inc., 1951.

Auerbach, Arnold, *Sculpture: A History in Brief*. London: Elek Books, 1952.

Barr, Alfred H., Jr., *Cubism and Abstract Art*. New York: Museum of Modern Art, 1936.

Barr, Alfred H., Jr., and Huguet, George, *Fantastic Art, Dada, Surrealism*. New York: Museum of Modern Art, 1936.

Barr, Alfred H., Jr. (ed.), *Painting and Sculpture in the Museum of Modern Art*. New York: Museum of Modern Art, 1948.

Basler, Adolphe, *La Sculpture Moderne en France*. Paris: Les Editions G. Cres & Cⁱᵉ, 1928.

Bitterman, Eleanor, *Art in Modern Architecture*. New York: Reinhold Publishing Corporation, 1952.

Bonfante, Egidio and Juti Ravenna, *Arte Cubista con le Meditations Esthetiques sur la peinture di Guillaume Apollinaire*, Venezia: Ateneo, 1945.

Bulliet, C. J., *Apples and Madonnas*. Chicago: Pascal Covici, Inc., 1927.

Cahill, Holger and Barr, Alfred H., Jr., *Art in America in Modern Times*. New York: Raynal and Hitchcock, 1934.

Casson, Stanley, *Twentieth Century Sculptors*. London: Oxford University Press, 1930.

Cassou, Jean, *Panorama des Arts Plastiques Contemporains*. Paris: Gallimard, 1960.

Cheney, Sheldon, *A Primer of Modern Art*. New York: Boni and Liveright, 1924.

Cheney, Sheldon and Martha Chandler, *Art and the Machine*. New York and London: Whittlesey House, McGraw-Hill Book Co., Inc., 1936.

Delevoy, Robert L., *Dimensions of the Twentieth Century. 1900-45*. Skira, 1965.

Dreier, Katherine S., *Western Art and the New Era*. New York: Brentano's, 1923.

Eddy, Arthur Jerome, *Cubists and Post-Impressionism*. Chicago: A. C. McClurg and Co., 1914.

Einstein, Carl, *Die Kunst des 20. Jahrhunderts*. Berlin: Im Propyläen-Verlag, 1926.

Fechter, Paul, *Des Expressionismus*. Munich: R. Piper & Co., 1920.

Fry, Edward F., *Cubism*. New York, Toronto: McGraw-Hill Book Co., 1966.

Gaudier-Brzeska, Drawing and Sculpture, with an introduction by Mervyn Levy. New York: October House, Inc., 1965.

Gaunt, William, *The Observer's Book of Sculpture*. London, New York: Frederick Warne and Co. Ltd., 1966.

Gertz, Ulrich, *Plastik der Gegenwart*. Berlin: Rembrandt Verlag, 1953.

Gertz, Ulrich, *Plastik der Gegenwart*, folge II. Berlin: Rembrandt Verlag, 1964.

Giedion-Welcker, Carola, *Modern Plastic Art: Elements of Reality, Volume and Disintegration*. Zurich: Verlag Dr. H. Girsberger, 1937.

Giedion-Welcker, Carola, *Contemporary Sculpture, An Evolution in Volume and Space*. New York: George Wittenborn, Inc., 1955.

Gleizes, Albert, *Vom Kubismus*. Berlin: Verlag Der Sturm, 1922.

Golding, John, *Cubism: A History and an Analysis, 1907-1914*. New York: George Wittenborn, Inc., 1959.

Goodrich, Lloyd and John I. H. Baur, *American Art of Our Century*. New York: Frederick A. Praeger (for the Whitney Museum of American Art), 1961.

Habasque, Guy, *Cubism* (translated by Stuart Gilbert). Paris: Editions d'Art Albert Skira, 1959.

A Handbook to the Solomon R. Guggenheim Museum Collection. New York: The Solomon R. Guggenheim Foundation, 1959.

Hayes, Bartlett H., Jr., *The Naked Truth and Personal Vision*. Andover, Mass.: Addison Gallery of American Art, Phillips Academy, 1955.

Hildebrandt, Prof. Hans, *Die Kunst des 19ten und 20ten Jahrhunderts*. Potsdam: Akademische Verlagsgesellschaft Athenaion, M.B.H., 1924.

Janis, Harriet and Rudi Blesh, *Collage: Personalities, concepts, techniques*. Philadelphia: Chilton Co.—Book Division Publishers, 1962.

Korro, Katarzyna and Vladistav Strzeminski, *Kompozycja Przestrzeni*. Lodz, Poland: Mazurkiewicz, 1928.

Kranz, Stewart and Robert Fisher, *The Design Continuum: An Approach to Understanding Visual Forms*. New York: Reinhold Publishing Corp., 1966.

Kuhn, Alfred, *Die Neue Plastik*. Munich: Delphin Verlag, 1921.

Larkin, Oliver W., *Art and Life in America*. New York: Rinehart and Co., Inc., 1949.

Levy, Mervyn, *The Artist and the Nude: An Anthology of Drawings*. New York: Clarkson N. Potter, Inc., 1965.

Lissitzky, E. and Hans Arp, *Die Kunst Ismen*. Zurich: Verlag Eugen Reutsch, 1925.

Moholy-Nagy, Laszlo, *The New Vision*. New York: Wittenborn and Co., 1946.

Moholy-Nagy, Laszlo, *Vision in Motion*. Chicago: Paul Theobold, 1946.

Ozenfant, *Foundations of Modern Art* (translated by John Rodker). New York: Dover Publications, Inc., 1952.

Pearson, Ralph M., *The New Art Education*. New York and London: Harper and Bros., 1941.

Peters, Heinz, *Die Bauhaus-Mappen. Neue Europäische Graphik 1921-23*. Köln: Verlag Christoph Czwiklitzer, 1957.

Ramsden, E. H., *Twentieth Century Sculpture*. London: Pleiades Books, 1949.

Read, Herbert, *A Concise History of Modern Painting*. London: Thames and Hudson; New York: Frederick A. Praeger, Inc., 1959.

Read, Herbert, *A Concise History of Modern Sculpture*. New York: Frederick A. Praeger, Inc., 1964.

Read, Herbert, *Henry Moore*. New York: Frederick A. Praeger Publishers, 1966.

Richter, Hans, *Dada: Art and Anti-Art*. London: Thames and Hudson, 1965.

Ritchie, Andrew Carnduff, *Sculpture of the Twentieth Century*. New York: The Museum of Modern Art, 1953.

Rosenblum, Robert, *Cubism and Twentieth Century Art*. New York: Harry N. Abrams, Inc., 1960.

Schacht, Dr. Roland, in Max Epstein (ed.), *Das Blaue Heft*. Berlin, 1923.

Selz, Jean, *Modern Sculpture: Origins and Evolution* (translated by Annette Michelson). New York: George Braziller, 1963.

Soffici, Ardengo, *Trenta Artisti Moderna*. Firenze: Valecchi, 1950.

Vikonska, Daria, *James Joyce, Parallel to Genial Ukrainian Sculptor, A. Archipenko*. Lwow: Ukranian Scientific Society, 1934.

Walden, Herwarth, *Einblick in die Kunst*. Berlin: Verlag Der Sturm, 1924.

Walden, Herwarth, *Expressionismus. Die Kunstwende*. Berlin: Verlag Der Strum, 1918.

Walden, Nell and Lothar Schreyer, *Der Sturm*. Baden-Baden: Woldemar Klein Verlag, 1954.

Weber, Wilhelm, *A History of Lithography*. New York, Toronto, London: McGraw-Hill Book Co., 1966.

Westheim, Paul, *Architektonik des Plastischen*. Berlin: Verlag Ernst Wasmuth, 1923.

Willrich, Wolfgang, *Sauberung des Kunsttempels*. Munich: Verlag J. F. Lehmanns, 1937.

Yale University Art Gallery, *Collection of the Société Anonyme: Museum of Modern Art*. New Haven: Yale University, published for the Associates in Fine Arts, 1950.

Zahn, Leopold, *Eine Geschichte der Modernen Kunst*. Berlin, Ullstein: Propyläen-Verlag, 1958.

(C) PERIODICALS

"Alexander Archipenko," *Der Sturm* (Berlin) March, 1921.

"Alexander Archipenko," *Sturm Bilderbücher II* (Berlin) 1915.

Apollinaire, Guillaume, in *L'Intransigeant* (Paris) 28 février, 1914.

Archipenko, Alexander, "Erläuterungen zu meiner Arbeit," *Das Kunstwerk* (Baden-Baden) 9/XII (Marz, 1959) pp. 15-21.

Archipenko, Alexander, "Nature the Point of Departure," *The Arts*, Vol. V, No. 1 (January, 1924) pp. 32-36.

Archipenko, Alexander, "Space, Light, Transparency," *Arts and Architecture* July, 1951.

Archipenko, Alexander, "The Spirit of Music in Sculpture," *Europa*, No. 1 (May-June, 1933) pp. 32-35.

"Archipenko at 74," *Time Magazine*, Vol. LXXIX, No. 1 January 5, 1962.

"Archipenko Bronzes," *Ameryka* (Published for distribution in Poland by Press and Publication Service, United States Information Agency), No. 31.

"Archipenko Bronzes," *Ameryka* (Published for distribution in Poland by Press and Publication Service, United States Information Agency), No. 62.

Brest, Jorge Romero, "Diez dibujos de Alejandro Archipenko," *Imagen* (La Plata, Argentina), No. 1, ano I 1944.

Buffet-Picabia, Gabrielle, "Matières Nouvelles," *XXᵉ Siècle*, nouvelle série, XXI Année, No. 13, (Nöel, 1959).

Bulliet, C. J., "Since Rodin: Archipenko to Establish His School This Fall in Chicago," *Art Digest*, Vol. XI (July, 1937) p. 24.

Cicerone (Leipzig), Vol. 15 July, 1923.

Dangers, Dr. Robert, "Archipenko in Darmstadt," *Weltkunst* July 1, 1955.

Del Marle, "Prolegomenes," *Art d'Aujourd'hui*, series 2, no. 3 January, 1951.

Devestil, Artus Cernik, (Prague), 1922.

"First Sculpto-cubist," *Art Digest*, Vol. XIII (February 1, 1939) p. 27.

Genius, (Munich), 3 Jahr. (1921) I.

Goll, Ivan, "Archipenko," *Action*, No. 5 October, 1920.

Guèguen, Pierre, *Art d'Aujourd'hui* (May-June, 1953). Special Number on Cubism in connection with Cubist Exhibition in the Museum of Modern Art, Paris and London.

Habasque, Guy, "Archipenko," *L'Oëil*, No. 78 Juin, 1961.

Halle, W. Fannina, "Kandinsky, Archipenko, Chagall," *Die Bildenden Kunst* (Vienna), 4. jahrgang, Heft 11/12 (1921) pp. 177-87.

Hordynsky, Sviatoslav, "The Art World of Archipenko," *The Ukrainian Quarterly*, Vol. XI, No. 3 (Summer, 1955) pp. 219-226.

Krauss, Félix, "Archipenko," *Norte* October 21, 1942.

Kuh, Katharine, "Landmarks of Modern Art," *Saturday Review*, Vol. XLVI, No. 16 (April 20, 1963) p. 54.

Lippard, Lucy R., "Heroic Years from Humble Treasures: Notes on African and Modern Art," *Art International*, Vol. X/7 (September 15, 1966) pp. 17-25.

Ma Aktivista Folyoiral (Vienna), 1921.

Mardersteig, Arnold, "Der Bildhauer Alexander Archipenko, ein Vorkämpfer der modernen Plastik," *Die Kunst*, 54. jahrgang, Heft 10 (Juli, 1956) pp. 172-4.

Mascherpa, Giorgio, "Le Cento Trovate del Picasso della Scultura: Alexander Archipenko, che espone a Milano, è uno degli artisti più revoluzionarî del '900," *Gente*, N. 47, anno VII 21 Novembre, 1963.

"New Day for Old Cubist," *Life (International)*, Vol. 32, No. 6 (March 26, 1962) p. 78-80.

Rzepecki, Nestor, "Archipenko Interview," *Pace* (Toronto), Vol. II, No. 3 (June, 1955) pp. 10-17.

Sangiorgi, Giovanni, "La Pittura Scultorea di Archipenko," *Civiltà Delle Macchine*, anno XI, numero 5 (Settembre-Ottobre, 1963).

Schacht, Dr. Roland; "Archipenko, Belling und Westheim," *Der Sturm*, 14 jahrgang, Heft 5 Mai, 1923.

Les Soirées de Paris, Sommaire du No. 25 15 juin, 1914.

Taillandier, Yvon, "Conversation avec Archipenko," *XXᵉ Siècle*, nouvelle série, XXV Année, no. 22 Nöel, 1963.

Ternovez, B., *Presse et Révolution*, Moscow, 1927.

Wescher, Herta, "Collage," *Art d'Aujourd'hui*, 1951.

Wiese, Dr. Erich, "Alexander Archipenko," *Das Kunstwerk* (Baden-Baden), Heft 8/9 (1950) pp. 67-69.

Wiese, Erich, "Neue Arbeiten von Archipenko," *Cicerone* (Leipzig), 4⁰ Jahrgang 20 (1928) pp. 197-200.

With, Karl, "Zu einer Büste von Archipenko," *Genius* (Munich), Jahr 3 (1921) pp. 17-19.

(D) CATALOGUES

(Unless indicated by asterisks, one-man exhibitions)

1912   Hagen. Folkwang Museum. "Lefauconnier Alexander Archipenko: Verzeichnis der im Museum Folkwang im Dezember 1912 Ausgestellten Werke." Introduction by Guillaume Apollinaire.

1913   Berlin. Der Sturm. "Alexander Archipenko: Siebzehnte Ausstellung." Introduction by Guillaume Apollinaire.

1913   *New York. 69th Infantry Regiment Armory. "International Exhibition of Modern Art" (Association of American Painters and Sculptors, Inc.) (Armory Show).

1920   Venice. XII Exposizone Internationale d'arte, "Mostra Individuale di Alexandre Archipenko."

1920   "Tournée de l'Exposition de Sculptures, Sculpto-Peintures, Peintures Dessins de Alexandre Archipenko." Préface de Maurice Raynal. 24 novembre au 10 déc.: Salle d'Exposition de la Libraire Kundig à Genève, 8 janvier au 8 février: Kunsthaus, Zurich. En 1920: Expositions à Paris, Londres, Amsterdam, Bruxelles, Athène, Berlin, etc.

1920-1   "Exposition International d'Art Moderne, Suisse 1920-21. Exposition d'Oeuvres de A. Archipenko." Expositions en 1921: New York, Berlin, Dresden, Munich, Dusseldorf, Frankfort, Paris. Préface de Maurice Raynal.

1921   Berlin. Der Sturm. "Alexander Archipenko. Skulpturen, Skulpto-Malereien, Aquarelle, Tuchzeichnungen, Bleistiftzeichnungen."

1921   Potsdam. "Alexander Archipenko. Retrospektive Ausstellung." Introduction by Ivan Goll.

1922   Frankfurt. Kunstsalon Ludwig Schames. "Alexander Archipenko, Elfte Retrospektive Ausstellung. Lyonel Feininger." Introduction by Wilhelm Hausenstein.

1923   Devetsily, Prague. Tekst Napsal Karel Teige Nakl.

1924   New York. Kingore Gallery. "The Archipenko Exhibition. Société Anonyme." Introduction and Catalogue by Christian Brinton.

1927   Chicago. "Tour of the Exhibition of the Works of Alexander Archipenko." Introduction by C. J. Bulliet.

1928   New York. The Anderson Galleries. "Archipenko. Catalogue of Exhibition and Description of Archipentura."

1929   Hollywood, California. Braxton Gallery. "The Archipenko Exhibition." Introduction by Harry Braxton.

1929   Chicago. The Arts Club of Chicago. "Alexander Archipenko."

1929   *San Francisco. The California Palace of the Legion of Honor, Lincoln Park. "Contemporary American Sculpture."

1929   New York. Saks-Fifth Avenue. "An Exhibition of Modern Sculpture by Alexander Archipenko."

1931   Hollywood, California. Braxton Galleries. "The Archipenko Exhibition."

1932   New York. John Levy Galleries. "A. Archipenko. Exhibition of New Works."

1933   Chicago. "The Archipenko Exposition of Sculpture and Painting" in Ukrainian Pavilion at "A Century of Progress," Chicago. Introduction by C. J. Bulliet.

1933   Santa Barbara, California. Faulkner Memorial Art Gallery. "Exhibitions: Sculpture, Painting and Drawing by Archipenko."

1939   Omaha, Nebraska. University of Omaha. "Alexander Archipenko in Retrospect."

1940   Cleveland, Ohio. Dedication Souvenir Program of the Ukrainian Cultural Gardens, Cleveland. "Inauguration of Three Monuments by Archipenko."

1942 *New York. "Art of this Century." Peggy Guggenheim.

1944 La Plata, Argentina. Museo Provincial de Bellas Artes. "10 Dibujos de Alexander Archipenko." Introduction by Félix Kraus.

1944 New York. Nierendorf Gallery. "Alexander Archipenko: Sculpture. Paintings. Drawings."

1948 New York. Associated American Artists. "40 Years of Inventive Sculpture by Archipenko."

1949 Hollywood, California. James Vigeveno Galleries. "Archipenko Drawings."

1949 Omaha, Nebraska. University of Omaha. "Alexander Archipenko."

1950 Brunswick, Maine. Bowdoin College Museum of Fine Arts. "Colored Drawings by Alexander Archipenko."

1952 São Paulo, Brazil. Museu de Arte Moderna, de São Paulo, "Desenhos de Archipenko." Introduction by Wolfgang Pfeiffer.

1953 *Paris. Musée National d'Art Moderne. "Le Cubisme, 1907-1914."

1953 Guatemala City. El Instituto Guatemalteco-Americano. "Una Exposicion de Dibujos del Escultor Norteamericano Alexander Archipenko."

1954 *Sweden. "Der Sturm" (Vandringsutstallning 132, Sweden).

1954 New York. Associated American Artists. "Archipenko: 110th Exhibition, 50 Years Production."

1955-6 Darmstadt, Mannheim, Recklinghausen, Düsseldorf, Freiburg, Berlin. "Alexander Archipenko: Plastik, Malerei, Zeichnungen, Druckgraphik." (Traveling Exhibition in Germany) Introduction by Erich Wiese.

1956 Indiana, Pennsylvania. State Teachers College. "Alexander Archipenko, Sculpture 1909-1955."

1956-7 *Vienna. Die Moderne Galerie Des Kunsthistorischen Museums. "Ausstellung in der Akademie der Bildenden Künste."

1957 New York. Perls Galleries. "Archipenko. Recent Polychromes."

1958 *Paris. Galerie Knoedler. "Les Soirées de Paris."

1958 *Brussels. "Exposition International des Beaux-Arts."

1959 *Padova. Sala Della Ragione. "XIII Biennale d'arte-triveneta: III Concorso internazionale del bronzetto."

1959 *Worcester, Massachusetts. Worcester Art Museum. "The Dial and the Dial Collection."

1959 New York. Perls Galleries. "Alexander Archipenko Bronzes."

1959 *Detroit. The Detroit Institute of Arts. "Sculpture in Our Time—Collected by Joseph H. Hirshhorn."

1960 Hagen (Karl-Ernst-Osthaus-Museum) and Münster (Freie Künstlergemeinschaft Schanze e.V., Münster Hauptbahnhof). "Alexander Archipenko: Plastiken, 1909-1959." Introduction by Erich Wiese.

1961 *Berlin. Schlosses Charlottenburg. "Der Sturm. Herwarth Walden und die Europäische Avantgarde Berlin 1912-1932."

1961 *Darmstadt. Hessisches Landesmuseum. "Bildhauer des 20. Jahrhunderts."

1962 Mannheim. Kunsthalle. "Alexander Archipenko: Zeichnungen, Aquarelle, 1912-1962." Introduction by Heinz Fuchs.

1962 *Köln. Wallraf-Richartz-Museum. "Europäische Kunst 1912."

1962 Winnipeg. Winnipeg Art Gallery. "Archipenko." Introduction by Ferdinand Eckhardt.

1962   New York. Perls Galleries, "Archipenko Bronzes."

1962   Dusseldorf. Galerie Wilhelm Grosshennig. "Alexander Archipenko: Plastiken aus allen Schaffensperioden."

1962-3 St. Gallen, Switzerland. Galerie "Im Erker." "Alexander Archipenko." Introduction by Werner Hofmann.

1963   *New York. Armory of the 69th Regiment, N.Y. and Munson-Williams-Proctor Institute, Utica, N.Y. "1913 Armory Show 50th Anniversary Exhibition 1963." (Sponsored by the Henry Street Settlement, N.Y.)

1963   Milan. Centro Culturale S. Fedele. "Mostra Antologica di Archipenko." Introduction by Giovanni Cappelletto.

1963   Rome. Ente Premi Roma. "Archipenko." Introductions by Giovanni Sangiorgi, Gino Serverini.

1963   *Washington, D.C. The Corcoran Gallery of Art. "The New Tradition: Modern Americans Before 1940."

1964   Munich. Galerie Stangl. "Alexander Archipenko: Ausstellung mit Skulpturen und Zeichnungen."

1964   *New York. Leonard Hutton Galleries. "Albert Gleizes and the Section d'Or."

1964   *Baltimore. The Baltimore Museum of Art. "1914."

1965   *Washington, D.C. National Collection of Fine Arts, Smithsonian Institution. "Roots of Abstract Art in America 1910-1930."

1966   *Houston. Houston Museum of Fine Arts. "The Heroic Years: Paris 1908-14."

1966   *Vienna. Museums des 20. Jahrhunderts. "Die Plastiken, Kataloge der Sonderausstellungen des Museums des 20. Jahrhunderts."

1966   *Albuquerque, New Mexico. University of New Mexico Art Museum. "Twentieth Century Sculpture."